"It is notoriously challenging to write a brief, thoughtful, one-volume introduction to the Bible. I commend the editors and chapter writers for succeeding admirably in facing such a challenge. They have written an exceptional text whose primary (but not exclusive) target audience will be undergraduate students enrolled in an introduction to the Bible class. Were I to teach such a course, this would easily be the volume I would use in such a class."

—**Victor P. Hamilton**, Asbury University

"This book is written by authors deeply committed to and engaged in both the life of faith (church) and the life of the mind (academy). They deftly weave the two together as they guide readers through the Bible. The inclusion of the intertestamental history and literature is a real gift and distinguishes this compact guide from even lengthy introductions to the Bible. If you are concerned with biblical illiteracy among Christians, this would be an excellent choice to give a solid grounding in God's dynamic drama."

—**Nancy R. Bowen**, Earlham School of Religion

"Many Christians, from college students to laypersons in Bible study groups, need a quick overview of the whole Bible to better understand this sacred text. These scholars have provided an easily understandable, comprehensive, and yet well-grounded introduction to the Bible. For those who read Scripture as God's Word for God's people, this is a very helpful book."

—**Scott J. Jones**, bishop, Great Plains Area,
the United Methodist Church

"Wall and Nienhuis have assembled a concise and readable guide to the Bible *as Christian Scripture*. This is not your typical historical and literary introduction but a guide to the Bible as the church's sacred canon. It is an outstanding resource for learning to read the biblical texts theologically and a gift both to the church and to the academy."

—**David F. Watson**, United Theological Seminary

"In a world where people go to war in the name of God and Scripture and where matters of law, morality, and ethics often lack foundation and context, a biblical people must master—and be mastered by—Scripture's story. This volume presents that story in a way [ ] us grasp its major themes and movements a[ ] for interpreting, assessing, and applyir[ ] it highly to those charged with comm[ ] whose lives should reflect the story, an[ ] story begs to be told."

—**David W. Kendall**, bishop, [ ] Church–USA

A COMPACT GUIDE TO THE WHOLE BIBLE

Learning to Read Scripture's Story

Edited by **Robert W. Wall**
and **David R. Nienhuis**

B
Baker Academic
a division of Baker Publishing Group
Grand Rapids, Michigan

Published by Baker Academic
a division of Baker Publishing Group
P.O. Box 6287, Grand Rapids, MI 49516-6287
www.bakeracademic.com

Printed in the United States of America

Library of Congress Cataloging-in-Publication Data
A compact guide to the whole Bible : learning to read scripture's story / edited by Robert W. Wall and David R. Nienhuis.
    pages cm
Includes bibliographical references and index.
ISBN 978-0-8010-4983-5 (pbk.)
1. Bible—Introductions. I. Wall, Robert W. II. Nienhuis, David R., 1968–
BS475.3.C655 2015
220.6′1—dc23   2014027923

15   16   17   18   19   20   21   7   6   5   4   3   2   1

Contents

Preface

This book originates out of a particular faculty's collective experience as teachers of undergraduates and adult Bible studies in local parishes. Like many other religiously related universities, Seattle Pacific University requires its students to take a survey course in Bible, most often during their sophomore year. Those of us who have taught this course over the years have found ourselves in a rather tight place. On the one hand, a survey of the biblical text requires more than simply reading the Bible. Students must be *introduced* to the Bible, for it is a huge book incorporating a rich and complex story. In order to enter meaningfully into the text, students require basic information about its nature and identity, its unity and diversity, its plotline and problems. There is only so much lecture time available in a typical class session, and few of us want to spend that time communicating basic realities that students really ought to encounter before class by means of a well-written textbook.

On the other hand, all of us wanted our students to spend the bulk of their time gaining experience in reading the Bible itself. What could be worse than a biblical studies course that spends all its time teaching readers *about* the Bible but never creates space for a deep, extended encounter with it? What we've needed is a short, accessible introductory textbook that would focus mostly on orienting readers to the *whole* Scripture in such a way that they are quickly enabled to pick it up and read the text for themselves.

And this has been the problem. The vast majority of introductory texts to the Bible provide, quite frankly, too much information. In the first place, most go to great length to introduce readers to a range of scholarly issues about the literary and **historical** background of biblical texts (terms appearing in boldface on their first appearance are defined in the glossary). We of course have no complaint about introducing students to critical issues. Our struggle, however, was to find a *short and readable* textbook that provided a relatively quick introduction to the Bible as *Scripture for the church*—as a book to be read and cherished by people in the pews; a book that is, by God's grace, accessible to everyone and not simply to scholars with specialized training in ancient languages and cultures. What we needed was a short "guide" of sorts that would provide just enough information to prepare the students to begin reading the Bible itself. Such a guide seems to us central to the educational mission of religiously related universities and Christian congregations.

After years of searching for the book we needed, we decided to write it ourselves. Apart from its obvious brevity, several features make this book distinct. First, because we believe the Bible was designed to function as Scripture for contemporary believers, this book begins with an extended reflection on what Christians believe about Scripture, and follows that up with a version of the Bible's **metanarrative** to help readers grasp the big picture of the biblical story. From there we introduce the biblical books according to the logic and sequence of their final form and not according to the various rearrangements provided by scholars who approach the text with a different set of (mostly historical) orienting concerns. For example, most introductory textbooks begin a study of the **Gospels** *not* with Matthew, where the New Testament begins, but with Mark, the agreed-upon earliest **canonical** Gospel; they read the Acts of the Apostles alongside the Gospel of Luke under the assumption that the two originated together and so must be read together, rather than reading Luke as the third of a fourfold Gospel and Acts as a bridge between the Gospels and letters; and they read the Gospel of John alongside the three letters of John (and sometimes even with Revelation) instead of as the culmination of the Gospel collection. Again, there is value in this sort of scholarly analysis, but we feel compelled to introduce students to the Bible they have received from the church, not the Bible they might have had if the ancient church had made different decisions during the **canonization** process.

Indeed, our format takes seriously the cues provided by the ancient church, which in the "fullness of time" formed Scripture for subsequent generations of its readers. Rather than present the material book by book, as though each biblical text existed in isolation from the others, our chapters introduce readers to the Bible's larger canonical subunits with an eye toward the "big story of the Bible" that holds all the pieces together: the Beginning of the Story (Genesis–Deuteronomy); the Story of Israel in (and out of) the Land (Joshua–Esther); the Witness of Israel's Poets and Sages (Job–Song of Songs); the Witness of Israel's **Prophets** (Isaiah–Malachi); Israel in Waiting (The Time between the Two Testaments); the Story of Jesus (The Four Gospels); the Story of the Church (Acts and the letters); and the Story's Conclusion (the Revelation to John). It has been our experience that this sort of narrative-theological approach best enables students to take hold of the importance of Scripture for their lives.

Each of the canonical-unit chapters unfolds according to the same structure. We begin by framing the books within the "big story of the Bible" with a section called "The Story: Contribution to the Metanarrative." This is followed by a section called "The Shape of the Story: Arrangement and Placement," which focuses on the "logic" of how the unit as a whole is sequenced. After that comes "The Style of the Story: Literary Features" to unpack the distinctive literary forms readers encounter in that unit, and each chapter is drawn to a close by a section entitled "The Specifics:

What to Watch For," which focuses mostly on theological questions. We are convinced that any encounter with Scripture should teach us about God's will and God's ways, so this last section addresses three pertinent questions to that end: What do we learn about God? What do we learn about being God's people? What do we learn about God's world?

As editors, we wish to offer our thanks to our colleagues in the Seattle Pacific University Bible department, who worked so hard to produce such a rich set of chapters, and to Nathan Sosnovske, our faithful editorial assistant who carried an especially heavy load on all our behalf. Thanks also to James Ernest, our editor at Baker Academic, whose invaluable editorial insights have improved the book immensely. Finally, thanks are owed to the students in our fall 2013 Christian Scriptures courses, who read initial chapter drafts and offered crucial feedback. If this book is able to reach its target audiences, both academic and congregational, it will do so in large part because we invited students to take part in the process of its production.

Robert W. Wall and David R. Nienhuis
Epiphany 2014

1

Reading the Bible as Scripture

Daniel Castelo and Robert W. Wall

This book is about reading the Bible as *Scripture*—the *church's* book, a *sacred* text. Our opening chapter seeks to set the table for the feast to follow, but not as most books like this one do. Those books introduce readers to the various strategies scholars use when studying the Bible as an anthology of ancient, religious texts. These are important matters, but first things first: the practices of biblical interpretation follow from the interpreter's core beliefs about what the Bible is. We have found that students need a compass to help navigate a pathway into the biblical text to mine its theological goods and assess their relevance for the life of faith today. This compass turns on what the church believes about Scripture.

There is good reason for us to begin the book here. Already in the seventeenth century, when science became the arbiter of enlightened truth in the West, the church's "Scripture" became the academy's "Bible." Scholars trained in biblical languages, literary art, and historical analysis became the Bible's most influential readers. They interpreted biblical texts by wrapping them up in ancient history and languages to explain the author's intended meaning for the texts' original readers in the ancient Near East (Old Testament) or Mediterranean (New Testament) world. This hard work continues today, and we understand the church's book better because of it.

To be sure, the positive purpose for doing the scholar's work was to protect biblical texts from self-interested, biased use of them—often by earnest Christians. But modernity's interest in what the Bible must have meant for its first readers created a vast distance between what the Bible meant in the past and what it means today for faithful readers who seek to hear a word from the Lord to guide their witness and form their faith. This same distance often characterizes the gap between the concerns of an academic study of the Bible and those of rank-and-file believers who receive this same text in worship and spiritual instruction.

By referring to the Bible as "Scripture," we do not intend to privilege certain interpretive methods as better than other methods; in fact, all the tools of modern criticism are used as God's gifts in due season. Rather "Scripture" signals a way of thinking theologically about the Bible as God's Word for God's people, one that supplies the theological goods that fund spiritual **wisdom** and provide moral direction (cf. 2 Tim. 3:15–17). Readers are cued that the rigorous study of the biblical text that they are about to undertake targets more than their intellectual formation; it offers them a fresh way of thinking about God and God's vision of a transformed people and a new creation.

Scripture Is Important

The questions we seek to address in this chapter follow from our core convictions about the nature of Scripture as a sacred text appointed by God to do holy work. The different roles Scripture performs in a congregation's worship and instruction, in our personal devotions, and in academic classrooms where biblical texts are rigorously studied should all logically follow from what we believe Scripture is.

In fact, this should be true of even the well-meaning skeptic for whom the Bible holds no religious importance. In this case, its texts are studied not for practical application to one's spiritual formation but out of deep respect for its importance for a particular religious community or in shaping Western civilization.

Our claim is that the Bible has always been much more than this for Christians. Jesus denied reports that he had come to abolish Scripture, claiming rather that the purpose of his arrival as God's Son was to fulfill the promises of God found throughout Israel's Scripture (Matt. 5:17–18). Christian readers approach Scripture the way that Christ does; they believe that what they find there discloses the full measure of God's promised salvation and then provides the hope that this salvation is graciously delivered by God's Spirit to all who believe in God's Son.

From its founding, the church has looked to the Bible to help believers understand their faith and guide their conduct in distinctively Christian ways. Christians believe that Scripture provides access to inside information about God. Studying the Bible is like entering a sacred place where the truth about God is encountered, which sometimes afflicts the comfortable and comforts the afflicted. God's biblical portrait gives readers a working sense of what practices and beliefs both please and displease God. Scripture is indispensable, then, in forming God's people.

At the same time, readers should always study Scripture with other resources that the Spirit uses to draw believers into loving communion with God. For example, Jesus followers have always disciplined their daily walk by worshiping together, praying for one another, practicing good works, and receiving the **sacraments** (e.g., the **Lord's Supper, baptism**) as the means of receiving God's empowering grace. Scripture's promise that where two or three are gathered in Jesus's name, his Spirit is there among them (Matt. 18:20) is made real whenever and wherever Christians gather together to worship God and the abiding presence of the Holy Spirit is experienced. At the same time, we should be mindful of the Lord's instruction for individuals to practice their daily devotions in private (Matt. 6:1–6, 16–18). While we hope this book guides Bible study in the classroom and congregation, we also hope it aids the individual reader to engage in what we happily call a "recreational reading" of Scripture!

Interpreting Scripture Is Hard Work

While Protestants have always granted a special place of privilege to the Bible, all Christians recognize that Scripture has the authority to teach them the ways of God. For some Christians, however, the Bible functions as the one and only reliable source for knowing God. Often this belief is justified by the perception that the institutionalized practices and traditions of the church have become faulty, unfruitful, and even unfaithful over time. These concerns have always been at the pivot point of Christianity's reform movements. The Protestant Reformers claim that "the church is always to be reformed" rings true even today, ironically even within some Protestant communions!

The deeply held sentiment that biblical teaching establishes Christian beliefs and practices has limits. Especially during the modern period, biblical scholars have become increasingly aware that a community's core beliefs *about* the Bible and its practices of *applying* the Bible are shaped by the concerns and experiences of a particular context. Without doubt, Scripture is an indispensable resource for Christians—when used in the company of the Spirit—for maturing in their understanding of the ways of God; it is, however, more than a mere philosophical foundation by which to build a fortress of timeless thought. Scripture is a holy text that must be interpreted and applied to ever-changing lives in an ever-changing world. God's Word is living and active, and the activity of interpretation helps make it so. The reader's work of adapting these precious but ancient texts to today's culture is no easy matter.

The reliance on Scripture alone to seek out the truth about God raises an important question: how is Scripture faithfully interpreted by all Christians in every generation of a global church? Interpretation is not a process of mathematical reasoning occurring in lockstep to arrive at the right answer. Texts are not puzzles or algebraic equations; they are collections of words that together form a meaning that relates God's Word to our lives. Interpretation is not only an intellectual exercise that requires knowledge of those "collections of words" but also an act of worship, requiring prayer and spiritual maturity that helps us adapt biblical teaching to daily life.

The Nature of Scripture

Scripture's importance and the hard work demanded of us to apply its teaching in formative ways are largely matters that recognize the special authority Scripture holds for a particular religious community. Christian theologians employ a wide variety of conceptions to describe and defend the importance of biblical teaching for the practice of Christian faith. Which among these conceptions provides the best account for Scripture's role in forming a robust faith?

Before we respond to this key question, remember what is at stake. The best way to protect a biblical text from a reader who mistakes or misapplies its teaching is to make certain that the content and consequence of biblical interpretation align with what the church believes about the Bible—about what it is and is not.

This entire book is organized by the straightforward conviction that the Bible is the church's book; it has special status and practical importance for every Christian. In part, this claim is based on a historical observation: there would be no Bible without the church that formed it (we believe under the Spirit's direction). But what we observe in the historical record is even more tightly secured by a theological understanding of Scripture as God's Word for God's people.

This integral union between the church and its Scripture leads us to suggest a particular rubric in describing its nature. Even as the Nicene Creed describes the nature of the church as one holy **catholic** and apostolic, these same four marks are also true of the church's book. Scripture is one holy catholic and apostolic text.

Scripture Is One

The Spirit works through both the Bible and the church to form an abiding witness of the goodness and beauty of God and God's purposes for all creation. In this sense, Scripture is "one" book not because it says the same thing in the same way; it is an anthology of many collections, written in many different literary genres and from different theological perspectives. The Bible's unity is a theological claim about its singular purpose to heal the world God created so that it lives, flourishes, and thrives alongside and in the presence of God.

To describe it as unified also recognizes that the Bible tells a single story whose central character is the one and only God. From Genesis to Revelation, Scripture witnesses to who God always is and what God has already done, is now doing, and promises to do in the future. Even though this plotline is neither a simple one nor one that follows a straight line, the Bible's story has a beginning, middle, and stunning end that tell the story of God's salvation in a comprehensive and coherent way.

Scripture Is Holy

When the Bible speaks of "holy" things, it refers to an ordinary someone or something that God appoints and enables to perform extraordinary roles among God's people. Sometimes people shy away from using the language of "holy" because it means for them that something or someone is flawless. We approach holiness differently. We believe the term applies to creatures of God's own choosing that God sets apart to accomplish God's purposes.

When we speak of the "holy" Bible, then, we are not describing it as a flawless book. Yes, the Bible is a thing of great beauty. But when biblical writers themselves describe the act of writing a biblical text (e.g., Luke 1:1–4), they describe an ordinary literary process of collecting and arranging materials, writing them down to serve the needs of their readers, so that what they have written will be received and read like any other story, poem, or letter. What makes the Bible holy—set apart for extraordinary service—is the Spirit's decision to select these particular texts, to guide the church in first recognizing these texts as indispensable for its future and then collecting them together to form a complete Bible (we call this "canonization"), and finally to illumine the church's use of Scripture for holy ends. Second Timothy 3:15–17 identifies these holy ends as the formation of spiritual wisdom and maturity that enables a people to know Christ and live like him.

Scripture Is Catholic

The Bible is a "catholic" book because it is "the Word of God for the people of God." The word "catholic" (small "c") means global and so refers to the scope of Scripture's influence, which extends to every culture in every age. If the church is global, so is every Scripture, which promises to communicate God's Word to every kind of Christian. The Bible is nondenominational!

Of course, the particular social contexts in which the Bible is composed, collected, canonized, and considered all matter. So do those real settings in which a particular congregation picks up the same Bible translated into its own language and receives it as God's Word. All interpretation is local interpretation! These contexts matter only in light of the conviction that every believer everywhere is "in Christ Jesus" (cf. Gal. 3:26–29). Each is a citizen of a new kingdom that embodies and shows the renewal of all things. The Bible is "catholic" because God uses it to establish God's reign on all the earth.

Scripture Is Apostolic

Those who are familiar with the Gospel story of Jesus know that he appointed some of his **disciples** as **apostles**. They were those who from the beginning heard, saw, and touched the historical Jesus (1 John 1:1–3). They knew him best and were witnesses to what he said and did as God's Son. Scripture is "apostolic" because all its teaching lines up with the testimony of these first witnesses of Jesus. Their story is our story. They are our trusted forerunners in the faith. Christians find their witness reliable and good.

When the Gospel writers tell their authorized biographies of Jesus, they do so with materials received from these apostolic witnesses who knew the historical Jesus best and who experienced firsthand the salvation he brought into the world. The New Testament letters are pastoral writings of these same apostles (or their associates). Even Paul, who never met the historical Jesus, was personally schooled by the resurrected Jesus (Acts 9:3–6; 22:17–21; 26:14–18; Gal. 1:12, 16; 2:2). And even as their apostolic witness and transforming experience of the risen Jesus were first interpreted by studying Israel's Scripture (our Old Testament), so now the church's book also includes the **synagogue**'s book. Both Testaments, Old and New, are apostolic in content and consequence. Israel's Creator God is the very same God personified by Jesus Christ, whom the apostles met, trusted, and followed. We trust the Bible's teaching as followers of Jesus just as his apostles did.

This last point leads us to the most important claim of all: if the apostolicity of Scripture assures its readers that its teachings are of a piece with the apostolic witness, then every good interpretation of Scripture will necessarily always focus readers on the risen, living Jesus. The church has always taught that all Scripture, both Old and New Testament, illumines his ways, which alone hold the key to our happiness—or to use scriptural language, Jesus is "the way, and the truth, and the life" (John 14:6).

A Few Good Questions

This book will not answer every question readers bring to the Bible. Its modest purpose is to provide an overview or framework of a particular way of thinking about the Bible that we hope will provide a way forward. But here are four good questions students constantly ask in the courses we routinely teach. We raise them in this opening chapter to illustrate how our understanding of Scripture carves out room for particular responses to familiar questions, which may also help readers see more clearly the Bible's enduring importance in their lives.

What Relevance Does the Bible Have for Its Non-Christian Readers?

The formation of Scripture (canonization) fixed a particular number of collected writings in a particular order to make clear their special significance in forming the faith and practices of Christian readers. But why should non-Christians be interested in stories that have no real bearing on a faith they don't share or a life they have no real interest in engaging?

First, if one accepts the Bible as a *cultural classic*, the citizen of the world may approach the Bible as a curious reader interested in a book that continues to exert power over the thinking and popular imagination of people, especially in the West. Even knowledge of the biblical story's plotline (see the next chapter) allows one to participate thoughtfully in a range of conversations about religion conducted in and for the public square.

Second, if one accepts the Bible as a *literary classic*, the well-educated reader may approach the Bible for the sheer pleasure that great works of art evoke. The appeal of its great stories, the memorable lyrics of the **Psalms**, the pithy wisdom of the Proverbs, the moral power of the Sermon on the Mount, and the arresting images of the book of Revelation have stirred the imagination of artists for centuries. Although Christians may not be disposed to think extensively about the Bible's literary artistry, it remains a good reason for non-Christians to enjoy reading and studying it.

Finally, if one accepts the Bible as a *devotional classic*, which every well-educated person should read, even the thoughtful non-believer may look to its depiction of the Triune God as a repository of spiritual wisdom that adds layers of meaning to the other sources of human wisdom, including the sciences and humanities. Any robust conception of a text's full meaning will include a spiritual dimension that complements and even helps to explain the material world. Even nonbelievers, for example, have found significance in the moral teaching and example of Jesus or in the cautionary tales of the kings of Israel told in the Old Testament.

Should We Take the Bible Literally or Figuratively (or Nonliterally)?

The question of whether we should take the Bible literally or figuratively is sometimes asked to disguise the more honest question: Is the Bible for real or is it just another religious fiction? People think that because a fiction never really happened, it has no relevance in the reader's search for truth. It has entertainment value but no theological substance. Yet this distinction does not match up with what we already intuitively know and experience. For example, the fictional drama *Les Misérables* has moved countless audiences to tears in the process of enriching one's appreciation for the beauty and tragedy of real human experience. The point was once made by a seminary classmate: "I would rather have a meaningful myth than a meaningless fact any day of the week." Myths, fiction, and stories are compelling because they convey significance and meaning about the human experience. The same is true with the Bible: its significance does not rest strictly on the historicity of all its claims. For example, the story of Job in the Old Testament, which begins with an otherwise unknown character located in the fictional land of Uz, seems to be a "once upon a time" kind of story. Yet there is hardly a more powerful biblical book about God's response to human suffering than Job's.

The story's opening makes it clear that his story is every reader's story. Of course, these determinations require great care on our part. If Jesus were simply a fiction and the resurrection a hoax, all else of Christian faith would fall by the wayside. Paul is right about this (see 1 Cor. 15)! But the question regarding literal or figural reading strategies usually assumes quite a bit about what counts as important knowledge, including what can be deemed as "true" or "false." The question often functions (mistakenly) as a test of one's devotion to biblical authority; however, Christians throughout history have taken the Bible seriously while reading it both literally and figuratively.

What Translation of the Bible Is Best?

The decision of choosing the "best" English translation of the Bible results in much hand-wringing, in part because such decisions typically take into account a range of personal preferences. But choosing one translation over another is an important decision. Every translation, after all, is an interpretation; for this reason, translators have labored to render the text intelligible for the contexts in which they have found themselves. Translation is a context-specific activity, and each translation carries with it certain aims and concerns.

This has always been the case. For instance, did you know that the version of the Bible that Paul used and called "God-breathed and useful" (2 Tim. 3:16) was a Greek translation from the Hebrew original? (Greek was Paul's first language and the language used in the Christian congregations he founded.) Accurate and readable translations are important in making Scripture accessible to the masses who know no other language than their own. But accurate and readable translations are also theologically important since they encourage regular use of Scripture by which the Spirit instructs and forms God's people.

Our suggestion is not to settle on a single translation, even though your instructor or pastor might recommend one in particular. Read two or three translations of the same passage to gain a better sense of the nuances and even significant grammatical and vocabulary differences, which often emerge in the process of translating the Bible into another language.

From Where and from Whom Did the Bible Come?

We have already said the church formed the Bible to help form the church, all under the direction of the Spirit. But we have said nothing about how, when, and by whom the Bible was formed. Unfortunately, a quick answer to this good question is impossible, because it requires the reconstruction of a long and complex history with large chunks of it unknown.

We do know that following their Babylonian **exile**, faithful Jews gradually produced two versions of their Scriptures, one in Hebrew and another in Greek (sometimes called the **Septuagint**). For the most part, the Greek version translates the Hebrew, but it would be a mistake to assume that where our current Hebrew text differs from our current Greek text the Hebrew readings are always older and better. The **Pentateuch** was produced first as Judaism's foundational text. Soon a collection of Prophets was finalized and placed with the Pentateuch to form the "Law and the Prophets." Later, a third collection of **Writings**, which included books of wisdom, a Psalter, and edifying stories, was added to complete the synagogue's biblical **canon**. The earliest Christian congregations often worshiped in Jewish synagogues and there were nurtured by Israel's Scripture from the beginning.

The Greek Bible, which was the primary translation used by the first Christians, is more chronological in shape and seems a better overall fit for the Christian Bible. Unlike the Hebrew Bible, which places its Prophets collection between the Pentateuch and Writings, the Greek version places its collection of Prophets last. When this ordering of the Old Testament is joined with the New Testament, an apt working relationship with the Gospels is created. When read together as a continuous whole, the Prophets immediately precede the Gospels as though creation's healing promised by God through the Prophets is now brought to realization by Jesus according to the Gospels.

More is known about the formation of the New Testament than the Old Testament because its history is far less complex in scope and more compressed in time. Yet again the central feature of this historical moment remains the gradual gathering of individual writings into collections that respond to the challenges that faced the early church (and still do). The church recognized the right shape of a particular collection (e.g., four Gospels, thirteen letters of Paul) by actually using these texts in worship and instruction. The texts that worked well were preserved, while those that didn't weren't. Biblical collections were assembled, not written. And they were assembled as they were read and put into effect within congregations, and then copied and carried down the road to another congregation and then to still another.

The years 200 to 400 CE were the pivotal years of canonization. The social forces that shaped the formation of the New Testament were mostly intramural, pitting one version of Christianity against another. The conflict between different groups of Christians provoked the following question: What version of the **gospel** is true? The Bible was formed as a Spirit-guided means to weigh competing claims and convictions about what it means to be Christian and to do as Christians ought.

Any answer to this question should not regard the Christian Bible as a loose collection of writings from which the reader may pick and choose to study one sacred text in isolation from the others. The Old Testament and New Testament form a self-contained and singular whole. The ancient rubrics "Old" and "New" imply Scripture's integral wholeness: there is no other sacred text needed to gain wisdom needed for salvation beyond this one book of "Old" and "New" Testaments to one God's single gospel.

Moreover, the different collections that make up each Testament were carefully fitted together into a specific order during the canonization process. For this reason, we think the initial pass through the Bible should be sequential—to get a good feel for the plotline of the Bible's story of God's salvation. If we believe that every biblical text is selected and inspired by God's Spirit for our theological understanding, their literary and theological diversity is reason for celebration, not disputation. Not only is it impossible to reduce the importance of any one part of the Bible as the only part that counts; the faithful reader relates the Bible's diverse witnesses together in ways that are mutually informing of God's full gospel. Only then does the church seek after a truly biblical understanding of God.

To Begin: A Theology of Scripture

Scripture has often been forced to fit what counts as true or respectable in any given age or social setting. But we have noted in this chapter that Scripture's interpretation must be Christ-centered, Spirit-led, and church-related in theological orientation and practical results. On this basis, two big-ticket ideas provide the beginning point of an intellectually and spiritually satisfying encounter with the church's one holy catholic and apostolic book.

If it were not for the Spirit and the church, there would be no such thing as a Christian Bible. The Bible does not just contain histories but itself has a history. This history involves the Spirit, who was active by providentially guiding the composition, transmission, collection, and use of these texts. The Holy Spirit used these texts to sustain the memory and proclamation of all that Jesus said and did. Also, the body of believers collectively known as the church has recognized certain texts as helpful in its task of mission and **discipleship**. This recognition is not strictly a human intellectual achievement; it is a worshipful and grace-laden development in which a Spirit-filled people come to recognize and know the ways of the Spirit so as to sense what does and does not contribute to the Spirit's purposes. Therefore, Scripture is a product of the Spirit working in the church to produce texts that can help this body as it grows toward God.

Only in the Spirit and in the church can one faithfully read the Bible as disciples of the risen One. Interpreting the Bible as Sacred Scripture is a spiritual activity; it beckons the Spirit's work of illumination. Words on a page or digital screen are just characters in and of themselves; as symbols, however, they signify and point to other realities. In the case of Scripture, its words signify and point to the self-communication of the Trinity. For this reason, believers need God in order to understand the ways of God. One cannot wade into the deep waters of Scripture apart from the prompting and guidance of the Holy Spirit. Additionally, if reading Scripture is a worshipful act rendered in and to God, then it is best pursued in the company of others who are striving toward that same end. An apprenticeship with wise practitioners of the Christian faith can help yield faithful readings of this text. Christians need to learn humbly and attentively how to approach this holy book before moving too quickly to apply it to their lives. This kind of worshipful apprenticeship, in the company of mature believers and the Holy Spirit, can help even the new believer gain the necessary maturity to study Scripture as the Word of God for the people of God.

| 2 |

Reading the Bible as Story

David R. Nienhuis

This chapter seeks to provide the reader with a short version of the story the Bible tells, the biblical "metanarrative." A narrative is, of course, a story—and the prefix "meta-" means (in this instance at least) "beyond" or "transcending." A metanarrative, then, is a big, overarching story that takes a group of smaller, different stories and provides a framework for understanding how they all fit together. As we will see, the Bible is made up of lots of different stories, but when we consider it as a whole we find there is a discernible overarching "big story," a "metanarrative."

There are, of course, some risks associated with the construction of metanarratives: because human beings are the ones who create them, they are unavoidably *contextual* (since they are told from one person's perspective and do not give us a God's-eye view), *reductionistic* (because they are a summary version of a huge story, so some things have to be left out), and therefore *contestable* (because different people will narrate things in different ways; one person's incidental bit, easily omitted, may be a central element in someone else's version of the story!). Worse, close attachment to one preferred version of the biblical metanarrative sometimes has the effect of *replacing* a desire to be intimate with the texts themselves. We must guard against this. A metanarrative is kind of like a map of the Bible; we *use* a metanarrative map to help us explore the biblical landscape, but we must never allow ourselves to think that possession of the map alone makes us familiar with the land itself.

Despite the risks, we cannot live without metanarratives. When we are unfamiliar with the biblical metanarrative, we lack a framework for understanding how the individual stories we read fit into the big story of God. What follows, then, is one version of that story.

The Beginning of the Story: Genesis–Deuteronomy

Before anything existed, the God of love and life was there. God's love burst forth in the form of a good and ordered creation, a world of life with which God might live in loving, trusting relationship— one where humans would truly know God and know what it is to live as blessed creatures in relationship with a loving and powerful Creator (the Bible uses the word **righteous** to describe this "right living" before God). Humans, however, turned away from God. Having refused the guiding hand of their life-giving Creator, the creation fell into disarray. As humanity multiplied and spread, God's good and ordered world became a place of *un*righteousness, characterized by alienation, disorder, violence, sickness, and domination. That is, creation became subject to the power of sin and death. But the God of love and life was still there, still bringing life into being and upholding the creation that was now damaged and in desperate need of repair (Gen. 1–11).

God launched a plan to conquer sin, repair creation, and make all things new. Because the God of love is essentially relational, God created a particular people group as a means of reaching out to the world, so that the whole creation might one day be restored to right relationship with its Creator. The plan was this: God would restore creation from the inside out, coming down to be made known through a particular group of people, empowering them to show the world both what God is really like and how it is that God wants people to live with one another.

Much of the Bible is given over to telling the story of that people group—the people of Israel. The story begins with Abraham and Sarah (Gen. 12), and follows God's blessing of their line through their son Isaac, his son Jacob, and in turn Jacob's twelve sons who would come to form the twelve tribes that make up the people of Israel (Gen. 24–50). The story goes on to describe their enslavement in Egypt and the powerful deliverance that God accomplished through a man named Moses. God saved the people by grace in order to make a **covenant** with them, to form them into a distinctive sort of people in the world (Exod. 1–15). God blessed them with a land in which to flourish and a set of instructions on how to live righteously (Leviticus–Deuteronomy) so that they might learn God's ways, turn away from their sin, and, in so doing, fulfill the task of showing the world what God is like and how God wants people to live with one another.

The Story of Israel in (and out of) the Land: Joshua–Esther

Right from the start, the people of Israel struggled to live in faithful relationship with their God. They failed to follow directions and often succumbed to the desire to be less like the people of God and more like the nations that surrounded them. God had to rescue them again and again (Joshua–Judges). Eventually God gave in to the people's desire to be like other nations and allowed them to have a king to rule over them in God's place (1–2 Samuel).

This growth in "worldly" power, however, simply resulted in an increasing lack of reliance on God. In the end, instead of becoming people who join with the Creator to help restore the world, they fell into the pattern of disorder and alienation that so plagues the created order. God sent a great number of messengers called "prophets" to remind the Israelites of their covenant with God, but the people continued their disobedient ways and were soon divided by conflicts. Indeed, the nation was torn in two to become a northern kingdom of ten tribes, called "Israel" (with **Samaria** as its capital), and a southern kingdom of two tribes, called "Judah" (with Jerusalem as its capital). While a few of these nations' kings were devoted to God, most weren't—and their collective unfaithfulness resulted in the ultimate destruction of both nations. Israel was taken by the Assyrians in the eighth century **BCE**, their people absorbed into that empire. Judah was taken by the Babylonians in the sixth century BCE, their people and wealth carried away into exile (1 Kings–2 Chronicles).

Ultimately the Persians, under the leadership of King **Cyrus**, conquered the Babylonians. Cyrus allowed the people of Judah (now known as "Jews") to return to their ancestral land. While they were allowed to rebuild God's temple and reestablish worship, they did not possess the land God promised to them, and they were not allowed to have their own king. The biblical story of Israel ends with God's people waiting and wondering how (or if) God would complete the plan to restore the creation through the people of Israel (Ezra–Nehemiah).

The Witness of Israel's Poets, Sages, and Prophets: Job–Malachi

Of course, it would be a great error to give the impression that all of the people in Israel's story failed to keep faith with God. During the "postexilic" period, God's people reflected on their story and reconsidered the witness of those of the past who had maintained faithfulness while the majority turned away. Soon the writings of Israel's great poets (Psalms, Song of Solomon), wise sages (Job, Proverbs, Ecclesiastes), and faithful prophets (Isaiah–Malachi)

began to be preserved and cherished by the people. God blessed
the reading of these writings, using them to inspire the people to
greater faithfulness and hope, and over time the people began the
process of gathering these writings together with the "beginning"
books (Genesis–Deuteronomy) as the holy Scriptures of Israel.

Israel in Waiting: The Time between the Two Testaments

For more than four hundred years God's people waited and
wondered. Eventually the Persians were conquered by Greeks,
who spread their language and culture through the lands they
possessed—a process called **Hellenization**. Jews of course kept
writing about God in this period, but now they were reading and
writing in Greek instead of Hebrew. **Scribes** therefore produced
a Greek translation of the Jewish Scriptures (which we now call
the "Septuagint," a Latin word referring to the tradition about
the "seventy" translators who took up the task). Others wrote
down stories of Israel's struggle to remain faithful to God while
living under the rule of foreigners (e.g., the books called Maccabees and the stories of Judith, Tobit, and Susanna). Still others
produced wisdom writings in the tradition of Proverbs (Wisdom
of Solomon and Sirach). While these later "Greek" writings were
incorporated into the Septuagint (which served as the Bible for
earliest Christians), Jews ultimately removed them from their collection of Hebrew Scriptures. Christians then and now have been
divided on the precise role these texts should play in the life of
God's people.

Israel also experienced a number of changes in its worship and
beliefs during this period. For instance, since there was no longer
a king, **priests** stepped up into leadership for God's people. Since
priests were in control, the Jerusalem temple began to take on
significance as the symbol of God's ruling presence in the world.
Since many Jews now lived long distances away from Jerusalem,
however, it became common to gather together in synagogues in

order to pray and to learn about God's Scripture from a rabbi (or "teacher"). It was into this world that Jesus of Nazareth was born.

The Story of Jesus: The Four Gospels

The faithful Creator's plan to restore creation could not be derailed simply because humans were unfaithful. But given the pervasive brokenness of humanity, what sort of action was required to restore our relationship with God? Who would show the world what God is really like, and who would be capable of showing the world how the Creator expects human creatures to live? There was only one thing to do: the Creator would have to enter into creation as a human creature; how else could one be capable of both revealing God's true nature *and* offering a demonstration of a human life lived rightly before God? So God came to earth in the person of Jesus, a Jewish male, an actual human formed of the same stuff as the rest of the broken creation and therefore susceptible to weakness and death just like the rest of us. Jesus proclaimed the "good news" about the God of love and life to his own people, and some began to follow him as their teacher and king. He gathered these "disciples" together as a kind of newly restored Israel who would be empowered to live according to his interpretation of Israel's Scriptures. In doing so, they would be enabled to take up the task that God laid on the people of Israel long ago.

The religious leaders of Israel, however, felt deeply threatened by Jesus's message—mostly because his teaching offended their religious sensibilities and endangered the power they held—so they decided that he must be destroyed. Rather than fight back or grab power for himself in order to save his own skin, Jesus gave himself up as a sacrifice, living his life righteously as a model of unwavering trust in God and devoted, loving service to others. He confronted the leadership in Jerusalem and was eventually arrested, tortured, and executed. He died and was buried in a tomb.

But this was no ordinary human being; this was the Creator in human flesh, the very Author of life itself, against whom even death itself has no power. Death, therefore, could not hold him; after he was dead for three days he broke forth triumphantly from the tomb, no longer as a creature subject to weakness and death, but as a "new creation," a human fully restored by God's life and love. After visiting with his disciples for a short time, Jesus returned to God, promising his friends that he would one day return but that in the interim they would be spiritually transformed to continue his work and model his pattern of human life in right, life-giving relationship with the Creator.

The Story of the Church: Acts and the Letters

The community of Jesus's disciples gathered together in Jerusalem after his death to pray and wait for God to act. A short while later God did indeed act by coming down yet again, not as a human being this time, but as a powerful indwelling Spirit who would live within and among God's new Israel, the church. Filled with the Spirit, this community became immersed in the power of life and love so that they too could do what Jesus did before them— that is, proclaim the truth about God and live together as newly restored creatures in accordance with the Creator's intentions for creaturely life (Acts 1–8).

The early leaders of the church took this good news about God's power of life and love out beyond the boundaries of Israel (Acts 9–28), starting new church communities in every region—inclusive churches made up of Jews and **gentiles** (non-Jews), slaves and free people, and males and females (Gal. 3:27–28). As they traveled about, they wrote letters of instruction and encouragement to the churches they formed, and these were eventually collected and distributed among the churches (the twenty-one letters of Romans through Jude). Though the churches were spread abroad and made up of many different types of people, all of them were unified by the Spirit as a new human community, a community who by word and deed would provide people with a glimpse of the "new creation" God has planned for the whole earth.

The Story's Conclusion: The Revelation to John

Throughout the story, God periodically provided certain people with hope-filled glimpses of what the creation will be like when everything is finally fully restored. One ancient writer of Israel described it like this:

> The wolf shall live with the lamb,
>   the leopard shall lie down with the kid,
> the calf and the lion and the fatling together,
>   and a little child shall lead them.
> The cow and the bear shall graze,
>   their young shall lie down together;
>   and the lion shall eat straw like the ox.
> The nursing child shall play over the hole of the asp,
>   and the weaned child shall put its hand on the adder's den.
> They will not hurt or destroy
>   on all my holy mountain;
> for the earth will be full of the knowledge of the LORD
>   as the waters cover the sea. (Isa. 11:6–9 NRSV)

This, then, is the final act in the story of God's creation, and it has yet to take place. Indeed, the Bible ends with a mysterious, symbol-laden story-poem of God's ultimate restoration of creation when Jesus returns in glory and the Creator gains the final victory over all that keeps the creation in bondage to the power of death. It insists,

> See, the home of God is among mortals.
> He will dwell with them;
> they will be his peoples,
> and God himself will be with them;
> he will wipe every tear from their eyes.

> Death will be no more;
> mourning and crying and pain will be no more,
> for the first things have passed away. (Rev. 21:3–4 NRSV)

The biblical story concludes, then, with an emphatic promise that, in the end, the faithful God will conquer sin, destroy death, and make all things right. Until then, God's people "follow [Jesus] the Lamb wherever he goes" (Rev. 14:4 NRSV), knowing that the journey will end in a creation fully restored.

Reading the Bible as Story

Chapter, Canonical Unit, Biblical Books	Major Plot Points and Characters
The Beginning of the Story *(Pentateuch)* Genesis, Exodus, Leviticus, Numbers, Deuteronomy	• Creation of the universe, humans, and their predicament (Genesis) • Ancestors: Noah (Gen. 6–10), Abraham, Sarah, and Hagar (Gen. 11–25), Isaac (Gen. 21–27), Jacob (Gen. 25–35), Joseph (Gen. 37–50) • Exodus: Slavery in Egypt, the call of Moses, and deliverance; journey through wilderness and receipt of the law at Mount Sinai; wilderness wandering (Exodus, Numbers) • The giving of the Mosaic law, transmitted in different ways across four texts: Exodus, Leviticus, Numbers, and Deuteronomy
The Story of Israel in (and out of) the Land *(History)* Joshua, Judges, Ruth, 1–2 Samuel, 1–2 Kings, 1–2 Chronicles, Ezra, Nehemiah, Esther	• Conquest of the promised land (Joshua) • Life in the promised land (Judges, Ruth) • Rise of the monarchy: stories of Samuel, Saul, David, and Solomon (1–2 Samuel, 1 Kings, 1–2 Chronicles) • Divided kingdom, north/Israel and south/Judah (1–2 Kings, 2 Chronicles) • Destruction and exile (2 Kings, 2 Chronicles) • Life after the exile (Ezra, Nehemiah, Esther)
The Witness of Israel's Poets and Sages *(Writings)* Job, Psalms, Proverbs, Ecclesiastes, Song of Songs	• Job: this story/poem about a righteous man who suffers innocently is an investigation into the meaning of suffering and the possibility of disinterested righteousness • David: traditionally the author of Psalms, though it is clear that many were not written by him (e.g., Pss. 68, 90, 137) • Solomon: As the one most closely associated with wisdom (1 Kings 3:5–15; 4:29–34), Solomon is the traditional (though not entirely actual) author of Proverbs, Ecclesiastes, and the Song of Songs (as well as the apocryphal Wisdom of Solomon) • Qoheleth: the "Teacher" or "Preacher" who speaks as the writer of Ecclesiastes
The Witness of Israel's Prophets *(Prophets)* Isaiah, Jeremiah (+ Lamentations), Ezekiel, Daniel The Book of the Twelve: Hosea, Joel, Amos, Obadiah, Jonah, Micah, Nahum, Habakkuk, Zephaniah, Haggai, Zechariah, Malachi	• The "major" prophets Isaiah, Jeremiah (+ Lamentations), Ezekiel, and Daniel proclaim to the southern kingdom its approaching exile due to sin, God's sustaining presence while the people are in exile, and the future salvation God has planned for their return from exile. • Hosea, Joel, and Amos collectively address the failures and downfall of the northern kingdom; Obadiah, Jonah, Micah, Nahum, Habakkuk, and Zephaniah prophesy the fate of the southern kingdom and surrounding nations; Haggai, Zechariah, and Malachi prophesy the restoration of Jerusalem following the exile.

Chapter, Canonical Unit, Biblical Books	Major Plot Points and Characters
Israel in Waiting *(Apocrypha/Deuterocanon)* Tobit, Judith, Additions to the Book of Esther, Wisdom of Solomon, Sirach (aka Ecclesiasticus), Baruch, Letter of Jeremiah, Additions to Daniel (Prayer of Azariah and the Song of Three Jews, Susanna, Bel and the Dragon), 1–2 Maccabees, 1 Esdras, Prayer of Manasseh, Psalm 151, 3 Maccabees, 2 Esdras, 4 Maccabees (note: actual order, content, and even titles of these books vary in Protestant, Roman Catholic, Greek Orthodox, and Slavonic Bibles)	
The Story of Jesus *(Gospel)* Matthew, Mark, Luke, John	• The preexistence of the Word (John 1:1–5) • Birth (Matt. 1–2; Luke 1–2) • Baptism and temptation (Matt. 3–4:11; Mark 1:2–13; Luke 3:1–4:13) • Gathering of disciples and public ministry (Matt. 4:12–25:46; Mark 1:14–13:37; Luke 4:14–21:38; John 1:19–17:26) • Passion and death (Matt. 26–27; Mark 14–15; Luke 22–23; John 18–19) • Resurrection (Matt. 28; Mark 16; Luke 24:1–49; John 20–21) • Ascension (Luke 24:50–53)

The Story of the Church
(Acts of the Apostles and Apostolic Letters)
Acts of the Apostles
The Letters of Paul:
    Romans, 1–2 Corinthians, Galatians, Ephesians, Philippians, Colossians, 1–2 Thessalonians, 1–2 Timothy, Titus, Philemon
Hebrews (anonymous)
The Catholic Epistles:
    James, 1–2 Peter, 1–3 John, Jude
	• The story of the earliest Jewish-Christian church in Jerusalem (Acts 1–15)
	• The rise of the Christian mission to the gentiles out of the Jerusalem mission, under the eventual leadership of Paul (Acts 9–28)
	• Letters written by Paul to churches (Romans to 2 Thessalonians) and individuals (1–2 Timothy, Titus, Philemon)
	• An anonymous Christian letter included in the Pauline collection (Hebrews)
	• Letters written by leaders of the Jewish-Christian mission in Jerusalem (James, 1–2 Peter, 1–3 John, Jude, called the "Catholic Epistles")

The Story's Conclusion *(Apocalypse)* The Revelation to John	• John of Patmos (Rev. 1:1–9) • The Christian churches addressed (Rev. 2–3) • The Lamb that was slain (Rev. 5; see also, e.g., 7:13–17; 12:10–12) • The woman, the child, and Michael the archangel (Rev. 12) • The dragon and the two beasts (Rev. 12–13) • Heavenly worship (Rev. 4; 7:9–17; 8:1–5; 11:15–19; 14:2–3; 15:2–8; 19:1–10; 21:1–4)

3

The Beginning of the Story

Genesis–Deuteronomy

Sara Koenig

The Story: Contribution to the Metanarrative

It is not surprising that this very first section of the Bible begins "in the beginning," when God creates the world. God creates a world of goodness and order, but God's good creation changes in Genesis 3, when Adam and Eve eat from the tree of the knowledge of good and evil and are cast out of the primeval garden of Eden. In the very next chapter, their son Cain murders his brother, Abel. But amid death, there is also life. God had commanded—and blessed—humans to be fruitful and multiply (Gen. 1:28), and the names of all of those who are born fill Genesis 5. The quick succession of generations slows down with the story of Noah, a righteous man in his time whom God commands to build an ark

to preserve animal and human life during a massive flood. After
the waters recede, God makes a covenant never to destroy the earth
again with a flood. Humans continue to be born, live, and die,
and their names are recorded in Genesis 10. A particular group
of people get the idea that they will make a name for themselves
by building a tower that can reach into the heavens. God decides
to confuse their language; when they are unable to communicate
with one another, they leave Babel unbuilt.

God promises to make a name for the character introduced next
in the story: Abram. In fact, God changes Abram's name, which
means "the exalted father," to Abraham, "the father of a multi-
tude." This name change is a reminder of God's covenant with this
human, a covenant that gets expressed in the threefold promise of
land, descendants, and blessing. Though God promises Abraham as
many descendants as the dust of the earth (Gen. 13:16–17), the stars
in the heaven (Gen. 15:5), or the sand on the seashore (Gen. 22:17),
this promise is endangered by the fact that Abraham's wife, Sarah,
is unable to have children. It takes a number of years before Isaac is
born to Sarah and Abraham, but after those years of waiting, God
tests Abraham by asking him to sacrifice that beloved son, Isaac.
Abraham passes the test, and Isaac—the child of the covenant—is
spared. Isaac goes on to have his own children, the twins Esau and
Jacob, and it is the younger son with whom the covenant is continued. Jacob has twelve sons of his own. After wrestling with God
(Gen. 32), Jacob is renamed "Israel." His twelve sons become the
twelve tribes of the nation of Israel. Jacob's favorite son, Joseph,
garners the jealousy of his brothers who sell him into slavery in
Egypt. But while Joseph is in Egypt, God uses him to preserve the
lives of numerous people during a famine that affects the entire
region. Those people include his own family, who come to Egypt
to seek food but who also find the brother they thought they had
lost. Genesis ends with Jacob's family in Egypt where they, like the
first humans, continue to be fruitful and multiply.

In fact, the fruitful multiplication of the descendants of Israel/
Jacob is so abundant that the new pharaoh becomes fearful of their

number and enslaves them. They cry out to God, who hears their cry and remembers his covenant with Abraham, Isaac, and Jacob. God calls Moses—who as a child was spared from death thanks to his mother, sister, and Pharaoh's own daughter—to bring the Israelites out of Egypt. Moses, like many of the people God calls, is fearful and reluctant. He eventually goes with his brother, Aaron, to tell Pharaoh God's request, "Let my people go, so that they can serve me" (Exod. 7:16; 8:20; 9:1, 13; 10:3). Pharaoh, not knowing God and reluctant to lose his workforce, refuses to acquiesce. God sends ten plagues, the last of which is the death of every firstborn in the land of Egypt. The Israelites are commanded to mark their doorposts with the blood of a lamb so that when God passes over, God will see the blood and not strike down their firstborn. At that first **Passover**, the Israelites left Egypt, freed from slavery and taking with them many of the possessions of their former captors. But though the plagues end, Pharaoh's heart is hardened and he pursues the newly freed Israelites into the Sea of Reeds, traditionally known as the Red Sea. God parts the waters so that the Israelites may cross through on dry land, but those same waters close over the pursuing Egyptians who drown in the sea.

Having escaped slavery, the people are led by God through Moses in the wilderness toward the land that had been promised long ago to Abraham. Immediately after praising God for God's deliverance (Exod. 15:1–21), the people start to complain about a lack of potable water (Exod. 15:22–27). While this is undoubtedly a legitimate complaint to make, it signals the people's lack of knowledge of and faith in the God who has **redeemed** them. God provides water to drink and daily food to eat (Exod. 16:12–13; Num. 11). God gives them the gift of the law, including instructions for **reconciliation** and restoration when they break those laws (cf. Exod. 34, the entire book of Leviticus, etc.). In fact, though the laws themselves are a different genre than narrative, they are an important part of Israel's story.

When the people are close enough, they send a group of spies into the **promised land**. Some of the spies report about the land's abundance: that it flows with milk and honey and has a single cluster of grapes so large that two men must carry it between them on a pole (Num. 13:23). But other spies bring an unfavorable report of the land, specifically that the Israelites will not be able to prevail against the strong, large people living in the land (Num. 13:31–33). Upon hearing this, the people respond with their most pointed complaint: they wish they had died in Egypt, and they make plans to return (Num. 14:2–4). God gets angry and tells them that they will die in the wilderness; only their children will enter the promised land after wandering in the wilderness for forty years. Still, God does not abandon them but remains with the people in such a way that even one who is hired by a foreign king to curse them can only, ultimately, bless them (Num. 22–24).

The final book, Deuteronomy, is set when the second generation—the children of those in Numbers—is about to enter the promised land. Moses reminds them of their history and reviews God's law, emphasizing that if they obey, things will go well with them in the land. If they disobey, things will go badly. Moses goes so far as to lay it out as a choice between life or death, exhorting the people to choose life by loving, obeying, and holding fast to God (Deut. 30:19–20). Because of Moses's own actions in Numbers 20, striking a rock instead of commanding it to yield water, he also is prevented from entering the promised land. Joshua is appointed as Moses's successor to lead the people of Israel. This section of the story ends with Moses seeing the promised land from the top of a mountain before he dies.

The Shape of the Story: Arrangement and Placement

As mentioned above, these five books begin the biblical text. In addition to providing the narrative of the beginning of the world, these texts are foundational for worship and theology. In Judaism, these books are authoritative for faith and life. In the synagogue, portions from these texts are read each week, with the entirety of

Genesis through Deuteronomy read each year. Within Christianity, these texts provide the foundation for theology about God, humans, sin, grace, and righteousness.

In addition to noticing how this section fits within the Bible as a whole, we also want to notice how the five books are arranged. The Greek name for this section of the canon is "Pentateuch," which means "five scrolls." Originally, texts were copied not on a codex with pages that turned but on a scroll that required rolling and unrolling in order to be read. The Hebrew name for this section is **Torah**, which is often translated "law," but a better translation is "instruction," as in teaching that gives guidance. Certainly the law provides guidance, but the stories also teach and guide through their positive and negative examples.

This section begins—appropriately—with Genesis, which is the Greek word for "beginnings." The Hebrew names for all the books in this section are taken from the first words in the Hebrew. In Genesis, the first Hebrew word is *bereshith*, or "in the beginning." The rabbis noted that the first letter, the Hebrew *bet*, is shaped so that it is closed to what comes before, and open to what comes after (it looks a bit similar to the letter *c*). Because of this, they suggested that we cannot know what happened before the beginning that is narrated in the text; questions such as "What did God do before creation?" are not answered by the text. Instead, our attention should move to what happens after the beginning. This section ends with Deuteronomy, a book that certainly does look forward to what comes next, as it ends with Moses looking beyond the mountain where he stands into the land that will be entered. In many ways, Deuteronomy can be understood as a boundary document. It is set on a geographical boundary between the wilderness and the promised land, and takes place on a narrative boundary when the Israelites have been led by Moses and are about to be led by Joshua. The book is also a canonical boundary between this section and the one that follows it.

In between Genesis and Deuteronomy is the giving of the law through Moses at Sinai, which begins in the middle of Exodus

(Exod. 19:1) and ends in the middle of Numbers (Num. 10:10). Therefore, the law accounts for half of the material of this entire canonical section. Additionally, the law is enveloped with the promise of the land: given to Abraham in Genesis, as mentioned above, and about to be realized with the end of Deuteronomy. In such a structure, we can see how obedience to God is the center of God's promises and their fulfillment. That is, the land is promised to God's people, but it is not something they are entitled to unconditionally. Instead, the stories of how God promised the land and how the people enter into the land are wrapped around God's directions for how the people are to relate to God and to one another.

The Style of the Story: Literary Features

Though there are a number of literary genres in the Pentateuch (including poetry, as can be found in Exod. 15; Num. 23–24; Deut. 32; etc.), the two main types are narrative and law. Genesis starts as a narrative, and that story continues through the first half of Exodus, when the genre then becomes law. The legal material then predominates through much of the second half of Exodus and most of Leviticus. Those legal sections are punctuated by some important stories, such as those of the golden calf (Exod. 32–34) and the death of Aaron's sons by the strange fire from the altar (Lev. 10). The book of Numbers begins with a census of the Israelite community, and the latter half of the book returns to narrative. The book of Deuteronomy is a narrative, but a complex one: it is told through the rhetorical device of Moses's speech. It includes both history and a retelling of the law to the next generation; the title "Deuteronomy" means "second law." Deuteronomy combines those laws that prescribe how the Israelites are supposed to live with sections of text that describe where they have come from. That sort of combination is characteristic of the entire Pentateuch, where story and law get interspersed and interrelated.

One literary issue that is distinctive in this section is the question of authorship. The traditional understanding is that Moses is the author of these five books (with some exceptions; cf. Num. 12:3 and Deut. 34:5–12). In the eighteenth and nineteenth centuries, German biblical scholars came up with a hypothesis that at least four different sources were responsible for either authoring the Torah or editing together texts that had been written by others. The "J source" used the divine name "Jahweh" to refer to God and tended to emphasize God's character as immanent and involved with creation (e.g., Gen. 2:4–25), while the "E source" used the divine name "Elohim" and often wrote about God as transcendent above creation (e.g., Gen. 20:1–18). The "Priestly source" was largely responsible for texts about the religious life and practices such as Leviticus, and the "Deuteronomist" produced, not surprisingly, Deuteronomy. These different sources are sometimes referred to by the acronym JEDP to reflect the chronological order of their writing, with the "J" material being earliest and the "P" material produced latest. They were thought to have been edited together into the final form of the Torah during the time of the exile or shortly thereafter, based on Nehemiah 8:1, which tells about the scribe Ezra reading from "the Torah of Moses." Noting these editorial realities has helped us to understand that claims of authorship are based less in history than in theological authority. That is, by referring to Moses as the one from whom the Torah came (in texts like Matt. 19:7–8; 22:24; Mark 1:44; 7:10; Rom. 10:5, 19; 1 Cor. 9:9), the faithful community could credit its authoritative teaching to its most authoritative teacher.

In addition to the overarching literary features of these five books, there are details worth noting in each book. For example, in the book of Genesis there is a repeated formula that introduces the generations (Gen. 5:1; 6:9; 10:1; 11:10, 27; 25:12, 19; 36:1, 9; 37:2), including the "generations" of the heavens and the earth (Gen. 2:4). In the book of Exodus, the ten plagues recur in a cycle that has the following pattern: God commands Moses to tell Pharaoh to release the people. Pharaoh refuses, and God sends a plague as threatened. Then the Egyptians cry out for relief, and Pharaoh and Moses have a conversation in which Pharaoh concedes that the Israelites can go. Moses intercedes and the plague ends, but then Pharaoh experiences heart hardening and refuses to let the Israelites go, which starts the cycle once again. These—and other—literary details make reading the Pentateuch all the more enjoyable.

The Specifics: What to Watch For

What Do We Learn about God?

One of the biggest challenges in reading the Bible is the idea that you already know what it says. This is particularly true for the first two books; those who plan on reading through the entire Bible cover to cover at least make it through Genesis and Exodus before getting bogged down—and possibly giving up—with Leviticus and Numbers. Or people have heard the debates over "creation versus evolution," and they assume they know "the biblical view" of creation. If you are one of those people, read it again. Read it slowly. Pay attention to what the text actually says and not simply to what you think it says or have heard that it says. You may be surprised by how God is described: more like a scientist experimenting with creation (cf. Gen. 2:18–21; 6:5–7; etc.) than a distant and omniscient deity.

In fact, seeking to understand more about God is the best starting point for approaching the topic of creation and evolution. Often that topic is presented in debate form, as mentioned above, where a person is expected to choose either creation or evolution. Admittedly, there are different methods for studying faith and science, and the disciplines think and talk in different ways. Also, the data is different, as is what it reveals: Scripture was written to reveal the nature of God, who is confessed to be Creator of heaven and earth. Data from the natural world bears witness to the science of natural selection. But Scripture and science can work together to point to the whole truth about the creation of life. Scripture, and the creation texts in particular, bears witness to God at work in the world. Science provides explanations of God's handiwork based on evidence found in nature. Neither task should detract from the other, but a careful study of both Scripture and science can offer the church mostly complementary tracks to truth, all of which belongs to God.

Because all truth is God's truth, we want to understand who God is, but in these texts God is complicated, unpredictable, and not always easily understood. For example, God is described as regretting making humans (Gen. 6:6); this is not some apathetic, unemotional God. In fact, God gets angry often. Even God's self-description as "slow to anger" (Exod. 34:6) comes right after God's anger is about to burn against the Israelites (Exod. 32:10) and God warns Moses that God might destroy the people (Exod. 33:3). In these texts, God punishes people often, and often in frightening ways, such as through fires (Lev. 10:1–3; Num. 11:1–3; 16:35), plagues (Exod. 32:35; Num. 11:33; 16:41–50), or the earth opening up and swallowing people (Num. 16:31–34)! But God's punishment does not cancel out God's care; in fact, punishment and provision are often juxtaposed in the text. When Adam and Eve were ashamed of their nakedness and attempted to cover themselves with fig leaves, God clothed them in garments made from animal skin. After Cain killed Abel, God put a protective mark on him so that the one who did such violence to his brother would not have violence done to him. One of the strangest things about the Old Testament is God, who cannot be reduced to a single action and who rattles the cages of our simplistic understandings.

What Do We Learn about Being God's People?

One of the important lessons of this Old Testament collection is that God's chosen people are not perfect. In fact, they are far from it, and as we look at their stories, we see jealousy, fear, forgetfulness, doubt, dishonesty, and dysfunction. Deuteronomy 7:7–8 expresses it succinctly:

> It was not because you were more numerous than any other people that the LORD set his heart on you and chose you—for you were the fewest of all peoples. It was because the LORD loved you and kept the oath that he swore to your ancestors, that the LORD has brought you out with a mighty hand, and redeemed you from the house of slavery, from the hand of Pharaoh king of Egypt. (NRSV)

In other words, God chose them not because they were the greatest but because God loved them and is faithful to God's promises. This particular reference points out another important lesson: God set them free from slavery because of God's love and promises, not because of anything they did. Notice the order; in the book of Exodus, the law is given to the people *after* they have been redeemed. God does not wait until they follow the law to redeem them. It was not as if God came to the Israelites and said, "Here's a list of the things you have to do and the way you need to live before I free you and make you my people. Once you show me that you can do these things and live this way, then I'll deliver you from Egypt." Instead, God's gracious act of **redemption** comes without preconditions or requirements. That's what makes it grace; it is not something earned. Then, after God saves the Israelites and sets them free, God makes known how they should live. Of course, this is the same pattern we see in the New Testament. Jesus Christ died on the cross to save all people from their sins. Paul's letters emphasize with crystal clarity that it is grace by which we are saved (Eph. 2:8–9), but once that has happened, the collection of New Testament letters known as the **Catholic Epistles** gives instruction for living a life of faith—doing "works." As James put it in his description of Abraham, "You see that his faith was active along with his works, and faith was brought to completion by the works" (James 2:22 NRSV). Thus, God's people are set free by God's graciousness and then given instructions for how to live.

Sometimes people stumble over how exclusive it sounds that God chooses a particular people group, as if that implies that God rejects others. But if we carefully read Genesis 12:1–3, we notice that God's call to Abram includes the assertion that "by you, all the families of the earth will be blessed." God does bless God's chosen people, but they are blessed—and chosen—to be a blessing to everyone else on the earth.

It is also important to understand the type of freedom God gave the Israelites. Too often, we think of "freedom" in the sense of autonomy or self-determination. But that was not the liberation experienced by the Israelites. The slogan of the exodus is summarized in the call to Pharaoh, "Let my people go!" But the fuller command reads, "Let my people go, that they may serve me" (Exod. 7:16; 8:20; 9:1, 13; 10:3). The Israelites were freed *from* their degrading subjugation to Pharaoh, but they were freed *to* serve the loving, redeeming God of Israel. No longer were they in bondage to the cruel, proud king of Egypt, but they were dedicated—even consecrated—to service to God.

God's chosen people are also holy people and are given laws that provide guidance for holy living. Jesus summarized the law by referring to two texts from this section of the Old Testament: loving God (Deut. 6:5) and loving neighbors (Lev. 19:18). Though "holiness" is a term negatively associated with legalism and judgmentalism, it is classically connected with being set apart and linguistically related to being whole. The Old Testament law expresses holy living not simply as some lofty theory—nor, again, as a precursor for God's grace—but as something that is made concrete when people treat one another with integrity, honesty, and justice. Even if we think today that humans can never be fully holy, holiness is presented as an inspiration and a goal.

What Do We Learn about God's World?

As the first chapter of the text affirms, God's world was created good (Gen. 1:4, 10, 12, 18, 21, 25, 31). Humans are closely connected to the rest of creation, as can be seen in Genesis 2 when Adam, the first human, was created out of the ground (the Hebrew word *'adamah*). In fact, human sin affects the created world: the ground is cursed because of Adam (Gen. 3:17–18). But after the flood, God states that God will no longer curse the ground because of humans (Gen. 8:21). Ironically, we humans seem to be the ones cursing the ground today. One of the implications of being created in God's image is that we humans are to care for the world. We notice that in the new creation, the world is not done away with, but includes a "new heaven" *and* "a new earth" (Rev. 21:1).

4

The Story of Israel in (and out of) the Land

Joshua–Esther

Frank Anthony Spina

The Story: Contribution to the Metanarrative

Joshua, Judges, Ruth, 1–2 Samuel, 1–2 Kings, 1–2 Chronicles, Ezra, Nehemiah, and Esther are often designated the "Historical Books." This title is certainly apt in that they ostensibly recount periods of Israel's history. Thus, Israel enters the promised land (Joshua; see Gen. 12:4–7), then lives in the land under a succession of **judges** and kings (Judges; Ruth; 1–2 Samuel; 1–2 Kings; 1–2 Chronicles), and then tragically loses but eventually returns to the land (2 Kings 22–25; 2 Chron. 36; Ezra; Nehemiah). The struggles of exiled Israelites living under persecution outside of the land are also highlighted (Esther). In this light, "Historical Books" seems harmless enough.

But there are also problems with this terminology. If these narratives are considered "history" in the sense of chronicling events, how should we categorize other narratives? Why would not the ancestral narratives (Gen. 12–50), the story of Egyptian bondage (Exod. 1–12), or even Gospel accounts be seen as historical? Why reserve the title "historical" exclusively for Joshua through Esther?

More important, since the so-called Historical Books are part of the church's *Scripture*, a word like "history" may actually be insufficient or even misleading. People for a variety of reasons may or may not be interested in a particular historical period. Medieval Europe or ancient China might excite while modern Canada or seventeenth-century Japan induce a yawn. In short, history as a category is something we take or leave depending on our personal experiences, intellectual interests, cross-cultural awareness, access to resources, and the like.

Scripture is different, though. Christians don't approach Scripture merely because of historical curiosity. Since Scripture describes how God acted through Israel and in Jesus the Christ to redeem, restore, and reconcile the created order, Christians find the whole biblical text compelling for spiritual, religious, and theological reasons. Granted, there are aspects of Scripture that may be considered historical, but ultimately Scripture goes beyond history. Because Scripture testifies to divine activity—historians deal exclusively with human activity—it might be more appropriate to think of biblical narratives as **transhistorical**. That is, Scripture certainly has a historical dimension, but it cannot be limited to that dimension.

As you know from the previous chapter, the first five books of the Old Testament describe how Israel became God's people and why. This story concludes with Israel in the wilderness listening to Moses's final sermons (Deuteronomy). Israel had yet to occupy the land God promised them. But once Joshua replaces Moses, Israel enters and appropriates the promised land (known as "Canaan").

After the Joshua generation, Israel lived in the land for a long time under judges. These judges, however, are not primarily legal figures but charismatic leaders who come forward at God's instigation in times of great need. During this period, Israel has devolved into persistent disobedience. Though Joshua depicts Israel as basically attentive to God's will (Josh. 1:7–8; 24:31), Judges portrays Israel as the polar opposite (Judg. 2:11–15). The extent of the disobedience is graphically illustrated by two horrific incidents (Judg. 17–21) that set the stage for the emergence of prophets and, eventually, kings (Judg. 17:6; 19:1; 21:25).

The book of Ruth follows Judges and precedes 1–2 Samuel. It explains the ancestry of David (Ruth 4:18–22), who became the Israelite king identified as the ideal "messianic" figure for God's people (**messiah** means "anointed"; "Christ" is the Greek rendering commonly found in the New Testament).

Though the books of Judges and Ruth prepare us for a king, 1 Samuel begins by describing the birth of Israel's prophetic ministry (1 Sam. 1–3). Biblically speaking, prophets precede kings. Once kingship is introduced (1 Sam. 8), however, Israel's ongoing story is narrated in the light of a long succession of royal figures. The largest section is devoted to the kingships of Saul, David, and Solomon (1 Sam. 9–1 Kings 11). After Solomon—and because of him—the kingdom of Israel is unfortunately split into two (1 Kings 11–12). From then on the saga of a divided people is narrated, until both kingdoms—Judah and Israel—end up in exile because of divine judgment (1 Kings 13–2 Kings 25).

First and Second Chronicles tell essentially the same story as that found in Samuel and Kings, but from a different viewpoint. Like the four canonical Gospels, which narrate the story of Jesus but with differing accents, so also 1–2 Chronicles re-narrates the story of Israel to provide readers with a different perspective. Though Chronicles proper concludes with the exile, the narration continues with Ezra and Nehemiah; these books recount the return from exile and a fresh start for the descendants of those who had experienced the humiliation of God's terrible judgment. The book of Esther provides one example of the sort of oppression to which Israel was subjected when living away from the promised land.

The Shape of the Story: Arrangement and Placement

The arrangement and placement of this collection of books narrating Israel's story is decisive in that its developing plot brings to the foreground a series of important theological issues for people of faith. Unfortunately, too many Christians remain woefully ignorant of several aspects of this portion of Scripture. Thus, our treatment of the story's "shape" calls for a detailed description of how one book leads to the next in order to communicate Israel's encounter with God.

To begin with, the book of Joshua must not be limited to a simple description of how Israel entered and acquired their land. The book sets the table for the whole canonical unit by setting up a command-obedience sequence: God commands Joshua, and Joshua commands the people (Josh. 1, esp. vv. 7–8). Joshua's obedience is implicit when he in turn commands the people, whereas the people's obedience is explicit (Josh. 1:10, 16–17).

Though the book of Joshua is often accused of being a text that glorifies militarism, military activity is actually downplayed. In fact, reading Joshua with a political or military lens simply distorts the text. To be sure, Joshua sends spies *secretly* (Josh. 2:1) before encountering Jericho, but this flies in the face of God's prior assurances (Josh. 1:2–6, 9; 2:1). Instead of gathering intelligence, the spies put Israel in the position of having to spare a Canaanite prostitute and her family in violation of God's command (Josh. 2:13–14, 19–21; cf. Deut. 20).

Furthermore, in the run-up to entering the land Israel marches behind a sacred vessel (called the **ark of the covenant**) as part of a miraculous crossing of the Jordan River, erects a pile of stones as a marker for future generations, circumcises every male under the age of forty (hardly a wise preparation on the eve of battle!), begins to eat the land's produce instead of manna, and finally marches around Jericho once a day for six days and seven times on the seventh day, at which time they shout and blow trumpets, which causes the walls of the city to come tumbling down (Josh. 3–6). Instead of a straightforward description of ancient warfare, the story draws attention to religious activities.

This emphasis is reinforced in other ways as well. For example, Joshua pits Israelites and **Canaanites** as polar *religious* opposites. Ironically, the most Canaanite character in the book—the prostitute Rahab—becomes, along with her family, part of Israel, while the most Israelite character—namely, Achan—is, along with his family, removed from Israel for his disobedience (Josh. 6:16, 23, 25; 7:1–26). The "outsider" Rahab ends up providing the best confession of faith in the book (Josh. 2:9–11) and ultimately becomes identified as an ancestor of King David and therefore Jesus as well (Matt. 1:5).

A glaring contradiction in the book of Joshua actually reinforces its role as Scripture rather than pure history. On the one hand, in a comprehensive summary statement we learn that every last inhabitant of the land has been eliminated in fulfillment of God's promise (Josh. 21:43–45). On the other hand, one of Joshua's final speeches to Israel warns Israel to avoid involving themselves with the Canaanites, neither interacting with them, nor intermarrying, nor acknowledging their gods (Josh. 23:6–12). Failure to heed this warning, Joshua insists, will lead to God's removing Israel from the land (23:13). But how can Israel intermingle with people who no longer exist? In strictly historical terms this is impossible, but at the literary level this is the point of the whole book. Joshua is about Israel's identity in religious terms, which explains Rahab's inclusion and Achan's exclusion. Henceforth, God's people are to obey God's law so that they do not fall through disobedience and idolatry.

Even the military aspect of Joshua should not be seen in conventional terms. Joshua himself makes this clear when he reminds the Israelites that their victories were not "by your sword or by your bow" (Josh. 24:12 NRSV). Indeed, when the Israelites acted contrary to their divine election they were themselves threatened with destruction (Josh. 7:12). Joshua has been shaped to ensure that Israel lives as Israel, not as Canaan.

Judges confirms this by concentrating on Israelite disobedience. Whereas the Joshua generation was obedient (Josh. 24:31), the Judges generation was not (Judg. 2:1–5). Thus, the victories noted in Joshua become defeats in Judges (Judg. 1:21, 27–36). This accent on Israel's sinfulness leads to a series of stories that are structured cyclically in a highly patterned manner. The cycle progresses as follows: (1) Israel commits evil; (2) the Lord punishes them by subjecting them to an enemy's oppression; (3) Israel cries out in agony; (4) the Lord hears their cry and raises up a judge as a deliverer; (5) the judge rescues Israel from oppression; (6) the land has peace for a time (Judg. 3:7–16:31). As though this pattern were not bad enough, each of the judges in the book is morally inferior to his or her predecessor. Even worse, the book concludes by relating two stories that show that Israel's depravity knows no bounds (Judg. 17–21).

Nevertheless, the way Judges is shaped evokes hope rather than despair. Every time Israel reels under divinely induced foreign oppression, they cry out. Each time, without exception, God heeds the cry and rescues the people. In other words, grace rather than judgment is God's final word. Though Israel is subject to divine judgment, God never completely abandons them. Throughout Judges, Israel is saved by grace.

Judges is followed by the development of Israelite kingship, but begins by telling the story of how the unlikeliest of characters—namely, Ruth—became an ancestor of David (Ruth 4:13–22). Ruth's identity as a **Moabite** (Ruth 1:4) typed her as the lowest of the low from an Israelite perspective, since the Moabites resulted from a scandalous incident in which Lot's daughters got him drunk and had children by him (Lot was Abraham's nephew; Gen. 19:20–38). This is yet another occasion whereby God uses an outsider to foster the future of Israel.

Though we have been prompted to expect the rise of kingship (Judg. 17:6; 18:1; 19:1; 21:25), 1 Samuel tells of the rise of prophetic ministry brought about by Hannah and her son, Samuel (1 Sam. 1–3). Yet despite Israel's recognition of Samuel's prophetic role (1 Sam. 3:20), they act as though he neither speaks nor exists in the very next episode, when they attempt to manipulate God (1 Sam. 4–6). After a space of twenty years, Samuel finally speaks and the people finally listen (1 Sam. 7). At last it seems like the prophetic ministry is on solid footing.

However, Samuel's age and his corrupt sons prompt Israel to demand a king "like all the other nations" (1 Sam. 8:1–5). Israel was permitted to have a king, but the king was to be oriented toward God and God's Torah (Deut. 17:14–20). Tragically, the sort of king Israel demanded of Samuel would lead to Israel's own oppression (1 Sam. 8:11–18). God had initially rescued Israel from bondage to a foreign king (Exod. 1–15), but now they were naively embracing servitude at the hands of one of their own. Despite Samuel's and God's displeasure, Israel's request is nevertheless granted. Still, Samuel predicted that the day would come when Israel would rue this fateful decision.

God selected Saul as Israel's first king, but that did not prevent disaster (1 Sam. 9–15). God also selected the next king, David; in many ways David was an improvement, but in the end he failed even more egregiously than Saul had (2 Sam. 11–12). But with David there was a difference. God decided that David and his offspring after him should embody Israelite kingship even if a particular king in this line was guilty of significant wrongdoing (2 Sam. 7). God was committed to the house of David in a way that God was not committed to the house of Saul (2 Sam. 7:15–16). But the canonical shaping of the material shows that this situation involved more than partiality on God's part. The final chapters of 2 Samuel are designed to present David as an ideal character; in fact, he was all but perfect (2 Sam. 22:21–25). Only this ideal king could serve as the model for Israel's anointed king, or messiah.

First and Second Kings illustrate how disastrous Israel's original demand for a king "like the other nations" was. David's son and successor, Solomon, took the throne through a struggle for power rather than through a divinely induced prophetic choice (1 Kings 1–2). Still, Solomon had an opportunity to combine wisdom and adherence to Torah to become a king in the pattern of the ideal David (1 Kings 3:5–15), but this opportunity was ultimately squandered. In fact, from the beginning Solomon was depicted as simultaneously wonderful and awful. In the end, Solomon's wealth, political power, and reputation were for his own self-promotion, notwithstanding achievements like building the temple in Jerusalem (1 Kings 4–11). Toward the conclusion of his reign, God raised up adversaries and prompted prophetic denunciations against Solomon (1 Kings 11:9, 14, 23, 26–39). The worst outcome of Solomon's kingship was the division of God's people Israel into two (1 Kings 12). Both thought at times they were the kingdom that truly represented God's elected people, but both invariably moved toward exile. The remainder of Kings moves back and forth between Israel and Judah, with famous prophets (like Elijah and Elisha) continually denouncing kings from both kingdoms for their failure to observe Torah.

Though Saul, David, and Solomon are perhaps the most famous Israelite kings, Josiah is described as the most significant ruler. Josiah was the king of Judah after the Assyrians had destroyed the northern kingdom of Israel (2 Kings 17; 22:1–3). The account of Josiah gets to the very heart of the nature of Israelite kingship. This king acted on the discovery of the apparently long-lost Torah to institute an extensive religious reform in Judah (2 Kings 22:3–23:25). He removed every trace of idolatrous religion and fostered practices and appointed personnel that were in keeping with the Torah. In fact, Josiah was the first Israelite king to celebrate Passover (2 Kings 23:21–23; cf. Exod. 12:1–28). These efforts earned Josiah unprecedented praise (2 Kings 23:25), marking him as the sort of king the Torah envisioned.

Alas, Josiah's efforts were too late to stay God's judgment. The king's death in battle demonstrated that Judah would suffer the same fate as Israel (2 Kings 23:26–30), and for the same reason: consistent and persistent sin. Thus Judah, too, was destroyed—in this case by **Babylon**—and many of its people exiled (2 Kings 23:31–25:26).

First and Second Chronicles bear a sort of negative testimony to our failure to take the Bible's canonical arrangement seriously. People may have a degree of familiarity with the material in Samuel and Kings, but know virtually nothing about the material in Chronicles. Why is that? The answer surely lies in the (mistaken) belief that Chronicles is simply a rehash of Samuel and Kings. If one knows the latter, why read the former? But this would be equivalent to ignoring Luke and John because one has already read Matthew and Mark. In canonical terms, 1–2 Chronicles has an outlook that is no less theological than that found in Samuel and Kings.

To be sure, 1–2 Chronicles covers the same era as that of Samuel and Kings, basically from King Saul to the exile. But its theological perspective is different in that the ideal of King David is highlighted from beginning to end. Indeed, David is portrayed throughout not only as Israel's ideal king but even as its ideal priest. This is illustrated by the many situations in which David makes certain that the Levites carry out the activities to which they were supposed to be dedicated according to Torah (e.g., 1 Chron. 13:2; 15:2, 11, 12; 16:4). Over and over David is portrayed as focused on matters related to Israel's worship of God.

This tendency may also be seen in David's installment of his son Solomon as his successor. In 1 Kings 1–2, Solomon becomes king by outmaneuvering—with the help of an apparently scheming prophet—his older brother in the context of palace intrigue with virtually no reference to God's will. But in Chronicles David sees to it that Solomon becomes king with appropriate ritual, priestly personnel, and liturgical instruction (1 Chron. 23:1–6). Equally, in Chronicles other kings in David's line are depicted as following Torah to the letter.

Nevertheless, the kingship also ends in disaster in Chronicles, but with a bitter twist. When King Josiah interferes in Egypt's conflict with another nation, Egypt's king delivered a message from God. In essence, the king said that Josiah should not get involved, because he would actually be opposing God's will if he did. Josiah dismissed his rival's warning, thereby losing his life in the process (2 Chron. 35:20–27). As was the case in Kings, neither Israel nor Judah could avoid judgment given the extent of their disobedience.

Chronicles also has an unmistakable prophetic perspective (e.g., 1 Chron. 29:29–30; 2 Chron. 9:29; 12:15; 13:22; 20:20; 21:12; 24:19; 25:15–16; 26:22; 29:25, 30; 33:15, 18). But unlike the ending of Kings, which leaves Judah in exile, Chronicles narrates the beginning of the people's return from exile (2 Chron. 36:22–23). Just as God had previously spoken through the Egyptian king (2 Chron. 35:22), God now acts through Cyrus, the Persian king. God commanded Cyrus to build a temple in Jerusalem.

Ezra and Nehemiah seize on the positive ending found in Chronicles to describe the seminal beginning of the postexilic community. First, there is the release of the people under Cyrus to erect the temple (Ezra 1–6). Then there is the initial reform of the community upon Ezra's arrival (Ezra 7–10). In Nehemiah 1–6 the community builds walls to distinguish itself from outsiders. Finally, Nehemiah 7–13 deals with the reordering of the community's religious life under Torah. Perhaps more than anything else, Ezra and Nehemiah put in bold relief that judgment is never God's last word. This material calls attention to the fact that God's people have a future.

The final book in the collection, Esther, makes the same point, and also enhances that future by establishing a religious holiday that is to be celebrated by all successive generations of God's people (Esth. 9:20–28). Though in one way Esther has a secular cast to it—God is never mentioned in the story—the canonical shaping is such that the celebration envisioned at the conclusion of the book (i.e., the Feast of Purim) emphasizes a religious reality.

The Style of the Story: Literary Features

The primary literary form of this particular part of the Old Testament is narrative prose, notwithstanding a sampling of poetry found throughout (e.g., Judg. 5; 1 Sam. 2:1–10; 2 Sam. 22:1–51; 1 Kings 12:16; 2 Kings 19:21–28; 1 Chron. 12:18; 16:8–36; 2 Chron. 6:1–2). This is what we would expect in the recounting of a huge dramatic story, which begins with Israel about to enter the land that God promised them and concludes when Israel returns to that same land after having been kicked out because of divine judgment. However, saying that the writers wrote in prose is like saying that Mozart composed music. The statement is factual, but it does not go far enough.

It falls short because these narratives have been so very exquisitely written. Many Christians have tended to miss this dimension of Scripture by reading superficially or abstracting the stories from textual details. In point of fact, the biblical narratives have been written to provide nuance, texture, drama, surprise, irony, color, and emotion. As such, these narratives—as we briefly noted above—may fairly be characterized as symbolic, metaphorical, figural, poetic, and typological. This is what makes them theologically compelling, spiritually penetrating, and religiously profound.

The primary reason for this style relates to the subject matter of the text, which involves God and God's people. Mundane, neutral, dispassionate, and technical language is insufficient for subject matter of this sort. Biblical writers obviously knew that the language they used needed to be up to the task of narrating a dimension of truth that transcends mere description. This is why the narratives are imaginatively written, allusive and suggestive, arresting and provocative, and sometimes even jarring or dislocating. We are used to thinking of the stories Jesus told in this manner. We need to realize that Old Testament narratives have been composed in the same vein as well.

The Specifics: What to Watch For

What Do We Learn about God?

Certainly one thing we can say is that God is thoroughly involved with God's people. That is, we learn about God by observing divine activity during Israel's life. God elected Israel for two reasons. One, it was God's inscrutable will to select and then commit to a people whose existence would be perpetual. God will not ultimately abandon the chosen even when God judges the chosen. Grace always prevails. Two, God formed a people through whom God would eventually bless "all the families of the earth" (Gen. 12:1–3). Given that purpose, God works tirelessly to sanctify the people for this sacred task. This accounts for constantly calling people back to Torah, whether on God's own part or through spokespersons.

We also observe that God's judgment should never be seen as the opposite of God's love and grace. To the contrary, divine judgment is a function of God's love and grace. God wants to make Israel holy not only for its own good but also for the good of the larger task at hand—namely, restoring, reconciling, and redeeming the whole created order. A God who does not judge is a God who does not care.

Equally, God has no trouble working with and through broken and flawed Israelites. This capacity on God's part may be viewed as **sacramental**. That is, God has the ability to transform human activity into divine activity, to make the ordinary extraordinary, and to make the mundane sacred.

What Do We Learn about Being God's People?

As for Israel, it was to be a "kingdom of priests and a holy people" (Exod. 19:6). As such, all the myriad details of everyday life were to be consecrated to Israel's calling and mission. Entering the land was not a real estate transaction or a military endeavor; it was oriented to the future God envisioned for God's people. Living under judges was not a matter of having chosen a particular political form; it had to do with judgment and then gracious restoration. The prophets were not merely a clerical class; they were the mouthpiece of God. This is why false prophets were especially condemned. The kingship was not simply imitative of an ancient secular reality; it was to become the basis for God's ruling through God's anointed, or messiah. The return from exile under God's guidance was more than a reversal of fortune; it spoke to God's future plans for God's people and those whom God's people would eventually bless.

These texts also underscore that Israel is not an abstraction; it is a real flesh-and-blood people. Christians have erred when they have viewed Israel as having simply been replaced by a non-Jewish church. To be sure, a nationalistic or political Israel is not the same as the people of God. This is why the modern state of Israel should not be naively equated with the chosen people. But Israel remains the elect people of God. The church's emphasis on adding gentiles to the community actually takes seriously the addition of outsiders to Israel found throughout the Old Testament (e.g., Tamar, Rahab, Naaman, the Ninevites). Thus, it is altogether proper for Christians to read this material as revelatory and authoritative for believers rather than as ancient history, or as background, or as merely illustrative.

What Do We Learn about God's World?

The world in which God acts and Israel lives is a *real* world. This is why every facet of existence is pertinent to what it means to be the people of God. In short, there is no such thing as a "secular" realm. Every mundane reality has a sacred dimension. Biblically speaking, we should not seek God in some otherworldly spiritual dimension but in the nooks and crannies of everyday life. The biblical God is transcendent and extraordinary, to be sure, but this same God is to be found in the ordinary world that Israel experiences on an everyday basis. In that sense, biblical religion is concrete, not abstract; particular, not general; in the fray, not above the fray. The story of Israel insists that we are dealing with a living God and an actual people.

5

The Witness of Israel's Poets and Sages

Job–Song of Songs

Sara Koenig

The Story: Contribution to the Metanarrative

As the introductory chapter on the metanarrative admits, one of the risks of a metanarrative is that it is reductionistic; some things must inevitably be left out. This section of the Bible—Job through Song of Songs—is most often left out of overviews because it does not neatly fit into the large story. One reason is that these texts are, for the most part, not narrative. Instead, they are poems, proverbs, and prayers that may seem extraneous to the plot of the larger story, similar to the way that the songs in J. R. R. Tolkien's *Lord of the Rings* were mostly left out of the recent movies—or just sung in the background—because they didn't fit into the plot. Often, these texts are categorized as human responses to God.

A second way in which this section does not fit neatly is that the content pushes at the boundaries. Theologically, the material pushes beyond the boundaries of the tidy and confined understandings about God. And yet the same two reasons that cause people to leave out these texts are the very reasons why this material must not be missed. Though there is a lot of power in telling stories, in narratives, there is also something powerful about the form of poetry. The poems (and proverbs and prayers) reveal particular truths through their very form. While there is plenty in the narrative itself to remind us that God is complex and resists our attempts to force God into a manageable box, this section of texts teaches us all the more to expand our expectations.

And yet, having admitted that these texts are not a narrative, broadly speaking the Psalms do tell a story about the gamut of experience of life with God. There are psalms that orient the people of God to who God is: a good God, who provides comfort, hope, security, and blessing for God's people. There are also psalms that bear witness to the experience of disorientation; psalms that lament when God is silent or absent; psalms that give voice to the anger, frustration, and fear people experience when God does not act as God is expected to. And there are also psalms that reorient people to God by giving thanks when God has acted beneficially. Every emotion is expressed in the Psalms, from the heights to the depths, which might be one reason why the Psalms have been used as the prayer book of the synagogue and the church for centuries.

Just as the Psalms express the gamut of experience with God, so do the texts known collectively as the **Wisdom literature**: Proverbs, Ecclesiastes, and Job. Proverbs presents an optimistic view of the world as orderly. In Proverbs, what happens makes sense because of clear "cause-and-effect" relationships; God blesses those who do good and punishes those who do evil. Ecclesiastes and Job, however, are more skeptical and radical: they illustrate the limits of human power to understand God or to control life through human actions. Additionally, Ecclesiastes and Job both deal with the vexing, pervasive question of why bad things happen to good people. There is no simple answer to that question—in life, in theology, or in these books—but Ecclesiastes and Job invite us to keep asking it. In fact, these texts not only give us permission to ask the hard questions, but they even guide us in doing so. In contrast with the view of God found in Proverbs—that God punishes those who have done bad things—Ecclesiastes and Job both show that righteous people suffer while wicked people get off scot-free. This is in contrast with the view of God found in Proverbs and in many other biblical texts, that those who are being punished by God must have done something to deserve it. Because so many texts hold this "conservative" view of God, it is all the more important to have Ecclesiastes and Job included in conversations about the metanarrative since they give examples of how we can ask questions about the experiences of life we see.

Song of Songs is also included in this section of the canon, though it is one of the books whose inclusion in the canon was once debated. A quick read through the content will most likely help you understand why there were some concerns. Its traditional title, "Song of Solomon," gives one indication of how it can fit into the metanarrative; it was originally understood as a poem written by Solomon to one of his many lovers. The title "Song of Songs" is a closer translation of the Hebrew, but also expresses a superlative: in the same way that "King of kings" refers to the most kingly king, "Song of Songs" means that it is the most supreme of songs. Another way Song of Songs has been understood is as an **allegory**, where "the lover" represents God or Jesus and "the beloved" represents the synagogue or the church, respectively. It can also be seen as a somewhat racy poem celebrating human sex and love. If it is read in that way, then the big story of God, God's people, and God's world includes affirmation that sexuality is a good thing.

The Shape of the Story: Arrangement and Placement

This section is not in the same order in the Jewish and Christian Scriptures, and the differences between the two help us understand different ways we can read them. In the Jewish Bible, the book of Psalms begins the section known as the *Ketuvim*, or the "Writings." It is followed by Proverbs, and then Job. This order shows how the more-conservative affirmations in Psalms and Proverbs are followed by the skepticism in Job, where the faithful titular character experiences deep suffering and loss. Additionally, many suggest that Job's friends represent the perspective found in Proverbs by insisting that Job must have done something to deserve all the pain he is experiencing. This order can therefore illustrate the problems with taking the perspective of Proverbs to its conclusion. Job is followed by Song of Songs, the first book of the collection known as the *Megillot*, or "scrolls," in Hebrew. The *Megillot* includes Song of Songs, Ruth, Lamentations, Ecclesiastes, and Esther. Thus, in the Jewish Bible, there is some textual distance between Job and Ecclesiastes.

By comparison, in the Christian Old Testament Job follows Esther. This order suggests that Job takes place during the Persian period, as do the preceding books of Ezra, Nehemiah, and Esther, but it also signals the beginning of the poetic books in the Old Testament. After Job the order of the books is Psalms, Proverbs, Ecclesiastes, and Song of Songs. Thus, in contrast to the Jewish Bible's more "orthodox" structure, in which the affirmations of Psalms and Proverbs are followed by the skepticism in Job, the Christian Bible reverses this, allowing the skepticism of Job to precede the conservatism of Psalms and Proverbs.

On the one hand, this could suggest that "the questions" that Job raises are followed by "the answers" in Psalms and Proverbs. On the other hand, a reader who has already read through Job might have in mind the question "What about Job?" when she or he reads in Proverbs that a person who is faithful to God will be sheltered and protected from any harm (cf. Prov. 19:23). In this order, the confident perspective in Proverbs that life makes sense and the world can be clearly understood is followed by Ecclesiastes, where there is despair and an honest admitting that life under the sun can be perplexing and feel futile. Admittedly, very few people read the Old Testament in order, but one who does so will get a particular perspective on righteousness and wickedness, punishment and blessing. Finally, the Old Testament grouping together of Proverbs, Ecclesiastes, and Song of Songs reflects the traditional belief that Solomon was the author of those three books. As we noted in the "Beginning of the Story" chapter, traditional claims about authorship often are more about theological authority than strict historicity.

Again, the canonical shape in both sets of Scriptures—Jewish and Christian—places these texts in conversation with each other. It would be dangerous to allow any single biblical text or perspective to shape our entire view of God or the world, because more truth can be found in a canonical dialogue than in a monologue. The truth of Proverbs needs to be in dialogue with the truth of the more skeptical Wisdom literature in order to more fully reflect how things are with God, God's people, and God's world.

The Style of the Story: Literary Features

As mentioned above, the bulk of this material can be categorized in the literary genre of poetry instead of narrative or prose. Poetry presents theology in a different way than either story or systematics does. In particular, the language of poetry is more open, allowing a kind of "play" with words that is not present in more rational or analytic literature. Poetry inherently expresses things with a certain level of ambiguity, and therefore allows for paradox, contradiction, multivalent levels of meaning, or even open-endedness. This might make some people nervous, particularly those who want or need things of faith and God to be concrete, certain, or "black and white." Others, however, appreciate the way that biblical poetry allows for some polyvalence regarding things of faith and even regarding God. Admittedly, poetry can be difficult. It requires its readers to use their imaginations. It can surprise, startle, and/or provoke. Perhaps poetry demands its readers to be more patient—and more careful—in reading and interpretation.

One of the specific characteristics of biblical poetry is what is known as "parallelism," in which the lines of a poem are placed in "parallel" with each other. For example, the lines in Psalm 24:1–2 proclaim:

> The earth is the LORD's and all that is in it;
> > the world, and those who live in it;
> for he has founded it on the seas,
> > and established it on the rivers. (NRSV)

In these verses, the term "earth" is in parallel with "world," the action of "founding" is in parallel with "establishing." These are not exact synonyms, but underscore and emphasize each other. Similarly, "all that is in it" is in parallel with "those who live in it" in verse 1, while "the seas" are in parallel with "the rivers" in verse 2. In that last example, both are bodies of water, though they are obviously of different types. The things in parallel are not always similar; there can be a number of other manifestations of parallels, such as the "antithetical" parallelism in Psalm 1:6, which presents the parallel terms as opposites:

> For the LORD knows the way of the righteous;
> But the way of the wicked will perish.

In general, the idea of parallelism is that the lines in biblical poetry balance each other, whether that balance is similar, opposite, or building toward a synthesis.

Another literary feature of poetry is its use of metaphor and simile. It is important to recognize these for their art and beauty, as well as what they evoke: descriptions of God as "shepherd" (Ps. 23:1), of the person in pain being "poured out like water" (Ps. 22:14 NRSV), of a "quarrelsome person" like "charcoal is to hot embers and wood to fire" (Prov. 26:21 NRSV). When reading metaphors and similes, however, two cautions are necessary.

First, it is important to remember that while a metaphor might evoke certain comparisons, it also has certain limits. For example, when the beloved's teeth are compared to "a flock of ewes" (Song 4:2; 6:6), the simile is meant to suggest that her teeth are white, and not that they make bleating noises. When God is referred to as a "rock" (Ps. 18:2), that suggests strength and security, not that God is an inanimate object.

The second, related, caution is that metaphors and similes are not meant to be taken literally. There is no literal flock of female sheep in the beloved's mouth. It may be more challenging to know how literally to interpret metaphors about God: is God an actual shepherd (cf. John 10:11)? Again, with poetry the reader must consider both *how* it means as well as *what* it means.

In addition to the general literary features of biblical poetry, each book has some specific literary details. One of those details unique to Psalms is the superscriptions, which are the words often printed in a smaller font under the number of the psalm, before the first verse begins. In the Hebrew, the superscription is included as part of the psalm's verses. These superscriptions give some context, and also identify the traditional author of the psalm. For example, the superscription for Psalm 3 explains it as a Psalm of David, when he fled from his son Absalom (cf. 2 Sam. 15). Though David is traditionally thought of as the single author of Psalms, there are other names mentioned in the other superscriptions, including Asaph (Pss. 50; 73–83), the Korahites (Pss. 42; 44–49), Solomon (Pss. 72; 127), and Moses (Ps. 90). While these superscriptions are helpful in making connections between a given psalm and a particular time and situation, no psalm is limited to that time or to that history. Rather, the content of the psalms speaks to universal human situations, such as the feeling of being in the pit (Pss. 40:2; 88:4, 6) or the feeling of being surrounded by enemies (Ps. 17:9). Indeed, many people throughout history have wondered why their souls are cast down and in turmoil (Ps. 42:5, 11), and a number of individuals over time have recognized that, with God as "my light and salvation," there is no one to fear (Ps. 27:1).

The individual psalms can also be classified into particular genres, with particular forms. One type is the "hymn of praise," which gives praise to God for who God is. These include two parts: the first is an introductory "call to praise," often expressed as a command such as "Praise the LORD!" and the second part gives the reasons God is worthy of praise. Contemporary Old Testament scholar Walter Brueggemann refers to these psalms as "psalms of orientation," which orient a person toward God by affirming God's identity as provider, savior, one who is faithful, and so on.

The second type of psalm is a "lament," which has the following elements:

1. It is directly addressed *to* God and does not just talk *about* God. For example, Psalm 22 begins with the very personal address, "My God" (Ps. 22:1).

2. There are very specific complaints. In Psalm 22, the individual complains that God is far away and seems to have forsaken the individual (Ps. 22:1); the individual is being scorned and mocked by others (Ps. 22:6–7); and the individual is being surrounded by evildoers and frightening enemies (Ps. 22:12–13, 16). Even if God already knows what is going on, there is something helpful for the human about giving voice to what is happening.

3. There are very specific petitions or requests for help, so the complaints do not simply become ways to "vent." In Psalm 22, the individual asks, "Do not be far away . . . come quickly to my aid . . . deliver my soul . . . save me!" (Ps. 22:19–21 NRSV). These are often based on a recital of what God has done in the past, or what the psalmist knows God can do (cf. Ps. 22:3–4, 9–10).

4. The psalmist vows to praise God after God has met the requests. On the one hand, these "vows to praise" can almost read like motivational clauses for God, as if to say, "If you

rescue me, I will praise you." On the other hand, they reflect a deep trust that God will do what is being asked (cf. Ps. 22:21–22).

5. These laments often end with a final song of thanksgiving, as in Psalm 22:27–31.

Brueggemann refers to these as "psalms of disorientation." The pain that humans experience when the world—and God—does not behave as they expect is incredibly disorienting, and these psalms provide a pattern to work through that. Though it may seem strange to end a lament with thanksgiving, it may be more possible after one is encouraged to voice the complaints, identify the specific requests, and remember the qualities that make God trustworthy. Again, not every lament ends with thanksgiving, and it is important to have the example of Psalm 88, which ends with the word "darkness" (NRSV). Still, the form can provide a way to direct lament to God, and not remain mired within it. Psalms of lament, or disorientation, are the most common type of psalm within the book, which can point to how frequent the need is to lament.

The third type of psalm is a "song of thanksgiving," which gives specific thanks to God for something that God has done. Its pattern consists of (1) an announcement of praise; (2) a summary of God's actions; and (3) a conclusion of praise. Brueggemann refers to these types of psalms as "psalms of new orientation," which direct the people of God back to God after God has acted on their behalf. While we are wise to beware of using a pattern or form too slavishly, the forms can help us better understand what we are reading in these specific psalms.

In the book of Proverbs, it won't be a surprise that one of the specific types of literature is a proverb, a short statement that expresses a belief or ideal. But there are also larger instructional speeches (e.g., Prov. 1–9), which give both positive and negative admonitions. These are set in the context of parental instruction to a child. Notice how both the father and the mother are teaching and instructing (Prov. 1:4); also notice how the final oracles are attributed to King Lemuel's mother (Prov. 31:1).

One of the overarching metaphors in Proverbs is that wisdom is personified as a woman (e.g., Prov. 1:20–33; 3:13–18; 8:1–9:6). This personification helps to emphasize the relational aspect of wisdom; instead of describing wisdom as an abstract concept or intellectual exercise, wisdom is a person who can be heard, with whom a meal can be eaten, who can be embraced. The final poem of the book, Proverbs 31:10–31, is an "acrostic poem," where each verse begins with the successive letters of the Hebrew alphabet. It has been interpreted in at least two ways, one of which is that it provides a blueprint for how women are supposed to act, which includes details like working within and outside the household. Another interpretation of this poem is that the woman described is Woman Wisdom herself, who appears throughout the book and also concludes Proverbs. A literary—and linguistic—detail worth noting in this poem is the way the adjective gets translated in 31:10: is it "capable," "excellent," "virtuous," or "of noble character"? The Hebrew word *chayil* means "strength" or "valor," as it gets used most often in the rest of the Old Testament in military contexts. This phrase, "a woman of valor," also gets contextualized in the story of Ruth, as Boaz uses it to describe her in Ruth 3:11. If the Proverbs 31:10–31 woman is meant to be an example for women, then Ruth provides a model of a biblical woman of valor.

Job is a text that combines poetry and narrative in a unique way: chapters 1–2 and 42:7–17 are a narrative, while chapters 3–42:6 are poetry. The character named as "Satan" appears only in the first two chapters and is not referred to at all in the poetry. The narrative is voiced in the third person, while the poems are written as a conversation between Job and his three friends Eliphaz, Bildad, and Zophar. The young man Elihu, who appears after the dialogues between Job and his friends have broken down, also speaks in poems, as does God when God appears to Job out of the whirlwind. The book of Job is a complicated and complex literary document, which fits the complicated and complex themes it deals with: the justice of God, the question of undeserved suffering, and what happens when orthodox beliefs about how God is expected to behave are challenged by human experience. Job may be the most challenging of all of the Old Testament books to cover in an introductory course, because when it gets summarized, it gets flattened.

Specific verses in the book of Ecclesiastes might tempt us to describe its overall perspective as pessimistic, such as, "I hated life, because what is done under the sun was grievous to me; for all is vanity and a chasing after wind" (Eccles. 2:17 NRSV). But for that very reason, it is important to pay attention to the overall structure of the book. This is not a neat, coherent, systematic text, but at eight times in the book, the author counsels the enjoyment of life (2:24–26; 3:12–13, 22; 5:17–19; 7:14; 8:15; 9:7–10; 11:7–12:1). This repetition occurs strategically throughout the text, often at the end of particular units. These encouragements to "joy" are all the more striking in a text that is so honest about the inescapability of death and the futility of much of the toil humans experience.

The Specifics: What to Watch For

What Do We Learn about God?

In 2003, cartoonist Bruce Eric Kaplan published a cartoon in *The New Yorker* that depicts God standing on a cloud, saying to a man standing in front of him, "I am big. It's the questions that got smaller." That single frame in many ways captures what these books tell us about God, who cannot be minimized in these texts and the questions they provoke.

There are so many descriptions of God throughout these texts, but three are worth noting. First, a number of times, in a number of ways, these texts teach that God provides. This message is particularly profound for those of us who live in a culture of scarcity. We don't have enough time, we don't get enough sleep, we worry about whether we have enough money to pay our bills, but these texts affirm that God not only provides but does so abundantly. Another often-repeated message is that God protects and delivers. Different metaphors speak to this theological affirmation: God is a shield, God is a fortress, God is a stronghold and a refuge. A third quality of God is God's power, but this quality can be both positive and negative. God's power to create, to rescue, and to punish the wicked is seen as a positive thing, but God's power is also frightening, particularly when it is directed against humans (cf. Job 9:1–19).

Another aspect of God that is highlighted in these texts, as a whole, has to do with God's presence and absence. The Psalms affirm that God's absence is fearful and painful, but Job experiences fear at God's presence. In fact, Job often uses the very language of the Psalms to make an overall point that is contrary to them (cf. Job 7:17–19; Ps. 8:4–5). When God finally answers Job from the whirlwind, those answers are not the simple ones that Job—or the readers—would like, but God is still relational with Job at the end of the book.

What Do We Learn about Being God's People?

On the whole, these texts are more focused on the individual than many other Old Testament texts, which are interested in the collective identity of Israel. These texts affirm that an individual is significant, that individual actions and choices matter. An overarching theme in these texts is that a person of God fears God. This does not mean that someone is afraid of God (though that may also happen) but signals respect and obedience.

These texts also give voice to many of the existential questions humans ask, such as, "What is the meaning of life?" "How can I live a good life?" "What effects do my actions have?" "How much control do I have over and in my life?" The different texts give different answers but collectively affirm that humans do want guidance and understanding in life.

Perhaps more than anything else, these texts affirm that matters of faith include our emotions and feelings, not just our intellect and logic. They also encourage God's people that every emotion can be expressed to God, taken to God. There is no pain that is too much for God, no despair too deep for God. In fact, these texts both provide a canonical affirmation that doubt and pain are primary to human existence and also give encouragement for joy and delight.

What Do We Learn about God's World?

Sometimes, there is a discernible pattern to God's world, and things that happen in the world make sense. Often, the pattern is opaque—or entirely hidden—and things do not make sense. Of course, both are true. As God describes the created world to Job, both death and life, violence and tender care, are woven into the world's fabric, sometimes at the same time (Job 39:29–30). The world is more frightening, more grand, and more profound than humans can understand, and God is present in it.

6

The Witness of Israel's Prophets

Isaiah–Malachi

Bo Lim

The Story: Contribution to the Metanarrative

What comes to mind when you think of a prophet? Someone who has supernatural powers who can predict the future? A campus radical who protests injustice and opposes those in power? In the Old Testament story of Israel, prophets are God's messengers whose primary duty is to call God's people to return to God and to announce to them the promise of salvation. They appear as important characters throughout the biblical story; Abraham, Moses, Samuel, Nathan, Elijah, and others, named and unnamed, are considered prophets in the Old Testament. But prophecy is not associated only with these individuals; it appears throughout Israel's Scriptures.

Jesus and his apostles, along with all those who wrote the New Testament, read the entire Old Testament as a prophecy that points God's people forward to fulfillment, when God's promises to Israel according to Scripture are realized through Christ (cf. Matt. 5:17; Acts 17:2–3; Rom. 10:4a). This chapter, however, considers a particular set of books collected under the title "Prophets" to serve a special role within Scripture. This collection includes Isaiah, Jeremiah, Lamentations, Ezekiel, Daniel, and the **Book of the Twelve** (the so-called Minor Prophets): Hosea, Joel, Amos, Obadiah, Jonah, Micah, Nahum, Habakkuk, Zephaniah, Haggai, Zechariah, and Malachi.

The prophetic collection doesn't tell a story but provides an inspired commentary on how God's people should understand the story narrated by the Pentateuch and Historical Books. They explain why things have turned out the way they have for Israel while at the same time providing a vision of hope for how things can change. While the Old Testament ends with God's people waiting and wondering how God's promise to restore Israel and redeem creation would be fulfilled, the placement of the Prophets collection at the end of the Old Testament points the reader forward to the New Testament and the proper conclusion of Israel's biblical story in the coming of Jesus Christ.

The Old Testament prophets minister during the last days of the northern kingdom of Israel in the eighth century BCE until Israel's restoration to the land following the exile in the fifth century BCE. The sweep of this story is plotted by 2 Kings, 2 Chronicles, Ezra, and Nehemiah; the Prophets collection should be read with these historical books open, since the one provides clues for how the other is read and applied.

In fact, the historical superscriptions of some prophetic books locate their messages within the biblical narratives of Israel's kings (cf. Isa. 1:1; Hosea 1:1; Amos 1:1; Zeph. 1:1). For example, the first verse of Micah situates its message "in the days of Kings Jotham, Ahaz, and Hezekiah of Judah, which he saw concerning Samaria and Jerusalem" (NRSV), which ties Micah to the story told in

2 Kings. The two books should be read together. Or another example: since prophets rose to prominence when Israel transitioned from a tribal confederacy (see Judges) to a kingdom ruled by kings, the earlier stories of how Samuel, Nathan, Elijah, and Elisha (cf. 1–2 Samuel and 1–2 Kings) are called upon to appoint or reject Israel's kings, to authorize war, and to confront the king's acts of idolatry and injustice provide biblical models of prophetic ministry that frame our reading of Isaiah to Malachi.

The backstory of the Prophets collection is a national calamity: the faithlessness of God's people results in their division into two separate kingdoms, Israel to the north and Judah to the south (cf. 1 Kings 12). In 722 BCE the northern kingdom is conquered by the Assyrians, the Israelite people are deported and resettled throughout the Assyrian Empire, and the northern kingdom ceases to exist (cf. 2 Kings 17). The southern kingdom of Judah resists Assyrian invasion and survives for another 136 years. During this time Babylon rises to power as the dominant empire in the ancient Near East and supplants **Assyria** as Judah's primary threat. Judah is eventually conquered by the Babylonians, and Judah's capital, Jerusalem, is destroyed in 586 BCE. Unlike the Assyrians, however, who made it their habit to disperse conquered peoples throughout their empire, the Babylonians resettled the surviving Judeans in Babylon. There the people of God live in exile until Babylon falls to the Persian conqueror Cyrus II. Beginning in 538 BCE, Cyrus allows the Israelites to return to Jerusalem and rebuild their city and temple. The books of Ezra and Nehemiah recall the journey home for these survivors, a diminished people from their former days, and their struggles to reclaim their city.

The Prophets collection provides commentary on the biblical story of a divided kingdom leading up to the Assyrian and Babylonian conquests, the trauma of Babylonian exile, and the challenges facing a greatly reduced Israel when it returns home but still under Persian rule.

The Shape of the Story: Arrangement and Placement

Scripture itself provides guidelines for interpreting the Prophets' message of God's unfolding plan for creation. The Prophets collection reflects what sometimes is called a "canon consciousness." That is, prophetic books were written and now are read with other Scriptures in mind; they demonstrate a keen awareness of earlier biblical texts through the use of allusion and quotation. The prophets make mention of persons and events in the other prophetic texts, or apply prophecies spoken in the past to later generations. For example, Jeremiah quotes a prophecy spoken by the prophet Micah a century earlier (Mic. 3:12 in Jer. 26:18). On another occasion Jeremiah adopts the message of Hosea, initially directed to the northern kingdom of Israel, and applies its central metaphor of God's people as a promiscuous wife to the southern kingdom of Judah (Hosea 1–3 in Jer. 2–3).

Prophecies do not operate according to a simple prediction-fulfillment scheme, but rather past events serve as the types or patterns of God's future action. We can envision God's future by the testimony of God's past. Prophets remind us that Scripture's witness to the history of God's salvation does not apply to a historical past but serves as God's Word for every generation that follows. So, for example, Matthew 2:15 can interpret the baby Jesus's escape to Egypt as fulfilling Hosea 11:1, "Out of Egypt I have called my son." Hosea makes no prediction but rather is describing Israel's past exodus. In what sense does Matthew rightly appeal to this Old Testament passage as a prophecy fulfilled by Jesus? Earlier in his prophecy Hosea announced that the future of God's salvation would take the same form as Israel's exodus (Hosea 2:15). Matthew picks up on this and so applies Hosea's interpretive key as his own: the arrival of God's salvation is cued by Jesus's exodus from a hostile Palestine to Egypt from where he will return or "come out of" to begin his work as Messiah.

It is important to note that the arrangement and placement of the prophetic books differs in the Hebrew and Greek versions of the Old Testament as demonstrated in the following charts:

Hebrew Bible

Law	Prophets	Writings
Genesis, Exodus, Leviticus, Numbers, Deuteronomy	*Former Prophets*: Joshua, Judges, 1–2 Samuel, 1–2 Kings *Latter Prophets*: Isaiah, Jeremiah, Ezekiel, Book of the Twelve	Psalms, Proverbs, Job, Song of Songs, Ruth, Lamentations, Ecclesiastes, Esther, Daniel, Ezra, Nehemiah, 1–2 Chronicles

Greek Old Testament

Law	History	Poetry	Prophecy
Genesis, Exodus, Leviticus, Numbers, Deuteronomy	Joshua, Judges, Ruth, 1–2 Samuel, 1–2 Kings, 1–2 Chronicles, Ezra, Nehemiah, Esther	Job, Psalms, Proverbs, Ecclesiastes, Song of Songs	Isaiah, Jeremiah, Lamentations, Ezekiel, Daniel, Book of the Twelve

The synagogue's Hebrew Bible possesses three canonical collections comprising Law, Prophets, and Writings. The Greek version of the Old Testament (the Septuagint), which became the Scriptures of the early church, is divided into four canonical collections: Pentateuch, History, Poetry, and Prophecy. The Prophets collection of the Hebrew Bible is further divided into "Former Prophets," which are included among the so-called Historical Books of the Septuagint, while the "Latter Prophets" form the Prophets collection of the Septuagint. Significantly, both Daniel and Lamentations are included in a third collection of the Hebrew Bible, called "Writings," but are included in the Prophets collection of the Septuagint and came to serve a prophetic role within the church's Scripture.

The differences between the Hebrew (synagogue) and Greek (church) versions of the Old Testament can be quite significant. For example, the book of Daniel is one of the most quoted Old Testament books in the New Testament, particularly by Jesus in the Gospels and by John in Revelation. It is fitting that Daniel is placed among God's Prophets in the Greek Old Testament, the one primarily adopted by the church, since it prophesies of Christ and the last days. Whereas the Hebrew Bible ends with the books of 1–2 Chronicles, the Greek OT concludes with the Prophets. In their current position just prior to the New Testament, the

Prophets contribute to a pattern of promise and fulfillment from Old Testament to New Testament in the canon.

The rubric "Law and Prophets" serves as an interpretive principle. Individual books were written and collected together with other collections in mind. One canonical collection ("Law," or the Pentateuch) should be read with the other ("Prophets") in mind. Modern scholars oftentimes drive a wedge between the two, viewing the Prophets as the originators of Israel's religion and the Law as a later development following from the Prophets. Yet the Bible is organized so that Law precedes Prophets. The final shape of the Prophets collection in the Hebrew Bible picks up on this nicely. Its opening chapter states, "This book of the law shall not depart out of your mouth; you shall meditate on it day and night, so that you may be careful to act in accordance with all that is written in it. For then you shall make your way prosperous, and then you shall be successful" (Josh. 1:8 NRSV). The collection's concluding chapter circles back to make this same point: "Remember the teaching of my servant Moses, the statutes and ordinances that I commanded him at Horeb [i.e., Sinai] for all Israel" (Mal. 4:4 NRSV).

Yet the Prophets collection is also conscious of the Bible's Poetry/Wisdom collection. Hosea, the first book of the Book of the Twelve, concludes with a statement regarding the importance of wisdom: "Those who are wise understand these things; those who are discerning know them. For the ways of the LORD are right, and the upright walk in them, but transgressors stumble in them" (Hos. 14:9 NRSV). This verse has the effect of linking the Prophets to the wisdom found in Job, Proverbs, and Ecclesiastes.

The Prophets are a collection of individual prophetic books. They are sometimes viewed as four collections of prophetic writings roughly equal in length. Because of their greater length, the church often refers to Isaiah, Jeremiah, and Ezekiel (along with Daniel) as "Major Prophets" and Hosea through Malachi as "Minor Prophets," since they are shorter in length. The influence of the "Minor" prophets on the church's theology, especially about the future of God's salvation, is hardly minor! While the Minor

Prophets can be read individually, they were compiled as a whole collection and read in the same way we read Isaiah, Jeremiah, or Ezekiel. In the same manner that readers appreciate the distinctive messages of each of the four Gospels (Matthew, Mark, Luke, John) but then learn to read them together as a fourfold whole, readers receive the distinctive witness of each of these four prophetic collections (Isaiah, Jeremiah, Ezekiel, Book of the Twelve) but then learn to read them together as a fourfold whole.

The Style of the Story: Literary Features

While the Old Testament prophets may seem bizarre to modern readers, they are actually quite conventional when considered within their own worlds. They spoke and acted in ways typical of ancient prophets so that their own audiences could understand their message. What holds prophets in common is that they all are intermediaries who facilitate contact between divine and human worlds. As *intermediaries* they serve as messengers of God to humans, intercede on behalf of humans to God, reveal things that are hidden to humans, interpret dreams, have visions of heavenly things, participate in the divine council, and uncover the schemes of humans. These various roles are somewhat represented in the different Hebrew titles of prophets in the Old Testament: *nabi'*, "prophet"; *ro'eh*, "diviner" or "one who sees"; *khozeh*, "seer" or "one who sees"; and *ish ha'elohim*, "man of God" or "holy man." It is no coincidence that two of these titles highlight the actions of prophets as seers, whom God enables with the capacity to find special significance in the ordinary. On several occasions God asks the prophets Amos and Jeremiah, "What do you see?" (Amos 7:8; 8:2; Jer. 1:11, 13; 24:3) and in each instance they "see" something they see every day: a plumb line, a basket of summer fruit, an almond branch, a boiling pot, and figs. God then reveals a word to the prophet for the sake of the people that grants special significance to these ordinary objects.

Prophets regularly *perform signs* to accompany their preaching. These signs are not necessarily miraculous; some are quite ordinary, others are bizarre, and some are outright scandalous. For example, Isaiah announces to Ahaz that a young lady will give birth to a child (Isa. 7:14); Jeremiah is told to purchase real estate even though the city will soon be overrun by foreigners (Jer. 32); Ezekiel is told to lie on one side for 390 days, the other side for 40 days, and eat bread baked over dung (Ezek. 4); Isaiah is told to walk naked and barefoot for three years (Isa. 20); and Hosea is told to marry and start a family with a promiscuous woman (Hosea 1). The purpose of these sign acts is to illustrate and verify the prophetic message. In the New Testament, Jesus and Paul are described in a manner similar to Israel's prophets; they too possess a divine commission and perform signs in support of their preaching.

Biblical prophets are *poets* not for artistry's sake but because poetry best serves their prophetic vocations. As one artist explains, "When something as catastrophic or cataclysmic comes as war . . . where lives are lost or [are] in jeopardy, the music steps forward to make the statement."[1] Prophets minister in times of crisis, when creative speech is used to break through and convince an unbelieving Israel that national catastrophe is imminent or to announce hope for a despondent people that their restoration is possible. The prophets see heavenly visions of **eschatological** judgment and salvation that they describe through vivid poems that help people imagine a reality beyond their human understanding. Israel's prophets are not doomsayers but focus on God's endgame: a new creation in which all the families of earth are blessed (cf. Gen. 12:3).

Prophetic literature includes all the forms of **Hebrew poetry**: parallelism, metaphors, similes, acrostics, chiasm, and word plays. Prophets are artful preachers who utilize the rhetorical tools of the trade, such as alliteration, **parables**, irony, and sarcasm. Prophecy is shaped by a wide variety of literary genres such as judgment

1. Peter, Paul, and Mary, *Carry It On—A Musical Legacy*, 80 min., Rhino Entertainment, 2004, as quoted in Louis Stulman and Hyun Chul Paul Kim, *You Are My People: An Introduction to Prophetic Literature* (Nashville: Abingdon, 2010), 3.

oracles, salvation oracles, oracles against nations, prophetic instruction, lawsuits, laments, hymns, love songs, and allegories. All
the diverse layers of poetic speech and literature create the intricate
tapestries of prophetic books that can be appreciated not only for
their individual parts but also as whole compositions.

Call narratives often play an important role in prophetic books
because they distinguish true from false prophets. The call narratives of Isaiah (Isa. 6), Jeremiah (Jer. 1:4–10), and Ezekiel (Ezek.
1–3) all resemble the commission of Israel's prototypical prophet,
Moses (cf. Exod. 3–4). Not only do call narratives authenticate the
divine authority of the prophet, they also define his sacred vocation.
For example, Jeremiah's call narrative concludes with God saying,
"See, today I appoint you over nations and over kingdoms, to pluck
up and to pull down, to destroy and to overthrow, to build and to
plant" (Jer. 1:10 NRSV). What distinguishes true prophets from false
ones is that they have access to the divine council (Jer. 23:16–22),
and these call narratives demonstrate that the prophet heard, and
could therefore preach, a heavenly message (e.g., Isa. 6:1–8).

Rather than form a continuous narrative, then, the Prophets
collection is best approached as an anthology of writings, even if
often linked to stories related to the time and place of particular
prophets. This may explain why this canonical collection seems so
haphazardly organized, why reading from its opening to concluding
oracle often takes the reader from one topic to another without
explanation—like a music album where each song possesses its own
vibe and lyrical line. Only when listening to the entire album does
one recognize that it forms a whole album of songs that maintains a
consistent yet multilayered theme (often cued by the album's title).

The Specifics: What to Watch For

What Do We Learn about God?

People are often drawn to the Prophets for their ethical instruction, and rightly so, but prophetic speech about God is more

creative and remarkable than this. Prophets encounter God and God's people in difficult circumstances, which often require them to push the boundaries of Israel's knowledge of God to provoke righteous responses. The various metaphors for God in the Prophets exemplify the confounding concepts of God found in this literature. They can be incredibly fierce and even frightening: God is a lion that roars and devours, or a warrior whose garments are soaked with the blood of enemies. Yet the metaphors can also be surprisingly tender: God is a heartbroken parent over a rebellious son, the nursing mother of an infant, or a distraught lover because of an unfaithful spouse. The Holy One of Israel is incomprehensible; Isaiah and Ezekiel each gaze upon God's glory but even then they can only manage to describe the features surrounding the throne rather than God's being. What is certain is that God is Creator and Redeemer and never abandons humans and creation. The prophetic word provides a word for people struggling to understand how a loving God remains committed to people even in the midst of tragedy and failure.

Much of the Old Testament assumes that Israel's God is supreme among other gods (e.g., Exod. 20:3); the Prophets collection clearly affirms monotheism, which denies that other gods exist, and the assertion of Israel's one and only deity is viewed as a reasonable act of worship. The Lord alone is worshiped; the idols of pagan nations are human inventions. Israel's God is the only Sovereign over all creation and the nations.

The Prophets maintain a tension between God's holiness, which demands a particular people's supreme allegiance, and God's love, which extends to all the families of earth. Whatever tension exists between God's love and holiness dissolves in God's self-description:

> The LORD, the LORD,
> a God merciful and gracious,
> slow to anger,
> and abounding in steadfast love and faithfulness,
> keeping steadfast love for the thousandth generation,
> forgiving iniquity and transgression and sin,

> yet by no means clearing the guilty,
> but visiting the iniquity of the parents
> upon the children
> and the children's children,
> to the third and the fourth generation. (Exod. 34:6–7 NRSV)

For good reason, then, the Book of the Twelve quotes or alludes to this passage on five different occasions (Hosea 1:6; Joel 2:13; Jon. 4:2; Mic. 7:18–20; Nah. 1:3) to witness to God's holy love and fair judgment of the guilty as well as extension of forgiveness to the thousandth generation.

Some prophecies include "sealed" visions of the last days that require a divine messenger to cipher their secrets (cf. Isa. 29:11–12, 18; Dan. 12:4, 9). In Jesus Christ the **revelation** of God's mysteries is made fully known. He is the prophet's word made personal (John 1:14) and through his ministry fulfills God's promises that the prophets foretell. Praise be to God that the Bible ends with its prophecy "unsealed" (cf. Rev. 22:10) and revealed through Jesus Christ. Prophecy is not to be set aside because Jesus fulfills it; Christian discipleship involves sustained attentiveness and obedience to the prophetic word. As Revelation promises its readers, "Blessed is the one who reads aloud the words of the prophecy, and blessed are those who hear and keep what is written in it; for the time is near" (Rev. 1:3 NRSV). The time that is near is the victory of God promised by the prophets.

What Do We Learn about Being God's People?

A great leader of the early church, Saint Jerome, summed up the Prophets this way: "In the Twelve Prophets we have the description as it were of a sick person who has refused to care for his illness right up to the point of death, and then the story of his healing after death by Christ, who is the true physician" (*In Esaia parvula adbreviato*; CCSL 73A:803.1–6). The Prophets collection addresses the collapse of the covenant between Israel and God. Isaiah opens with God's indictment of Jerusalem, Jeremiah

follows by announcing that an exile is imminent, Ezekiel then
predicts Judah's Babylonian exile, while Hosea, the first of the
Minor Prophets, announces that Israel is no longer God's people
and the Lord is no longer Israel's covenant God.

Yet all the prophets, each in their own manner and idiom, announce the coming of a new people that will experience far more
of God's blessing than the old. Isaiah speaks of a new Jerusalem,
a new creation, and a new exodus. The priestly prophet, Ezekiel,
emphasizes the religious aspects of Israel's faith, prophesying a
new temple, a new heart, and a new spirit for God's covenant
community. Jeremiah, who follows the teaching of Deuteronomy,
proclaims the arrival of a new covenant in which the law will no
longer be written in stone but on the heart. Covenant keeping will
be the new DNA of God's people. In the kingdom that comes with
the messiah, a righteous king of the kind promised to David (cf.
2 Sam. 7) will reign from the new Jerusalem to extend God's justice
and righteousness to all the families who populate the new creation.

But first the anti-God order of the old creation must come to
an end. Salvation will come but only after the discipline of judgment. In the Prophets, judgment and salvation serve as two sides
of the same coin of God's transformative work in the world. For
example, a unifying theme of the Book of the Twelve is the day of
the Lord. This motif appears in all but two of the Minor Prophets,
yet each occurrence of it can mean something completely opposite.
Depending on the context, the day of the Lord can signify God's
salvation (cf. Joel 3:1–2) or judgment (cf. Amos 5:18).

What Do We Learn about God's World?

Since the Prophets announce that the Lord is the true Sovereign
of the nations, all humans—whether Jew or gentile, leaders or
commoners, rich or poor, or male and female—are held ethically
accountable to God. The Prophets indict Israel and the nations for
their acts of violence, immorality, idolatry, social injustice, greed,
pride, and political treachery and call them to repentance. Israel

is to resist the seduction of foreign empires whose wealth, power, and idolatry constantly served as a temptation for Israel's leaders to compromise their belief that the Lord alone would provide for their security and well-being. Societies are evaluated by their treatment of the most vulnerable in their midst; of particular concern to the Prophets are the poor and marginalized. Israel's God is not parochial but is Lord of the nations; and therefore God judges the nations for their sins against humanity and creation, uses them to accomplish divine plans, extends mercy to them when they repent, and extends salvation to them through Israel, God's servant. The Prophets provide a model of living as faithful witnesses amid oppression and empire; they teach how God's people are to be "in the world, but not of it" even when they live on the margins of society.

| 7 |

Israel in Waiting

The Time between the Two Testaments

Chad Marshall

This chapter focuses on the story of Israel from the time of the second temple's construction in the sixth century BCE to its destruction in 70 CE. Called the **intertestamental period,** this portion of Israel's story sometimes gets overlooked in discussions of the Bible's metanarrative.

Perhaps one reason for this is the structure of the biblical canon. Unlike the Jewish canon, which ends with 1–2 Chronicles, Protestant and Catholic Old Testaments end with Malachi's prophecy that God will one day send Elijah to "turn the hearts of parents to their children and the hearts of children to their parents" (Mal. 4:5–6 NRSV). This ending helps give the Old Testament the sense of a story in search of a conclusion, which is then found in the very next portion of Scripture. At the beginning of Jesus's story in the New Testament Gospels, the angel of the Lord uses Malachi's prophecy to announce the imminent birth of John the Baptist: "With the spirit and power of Elijah he will go before him, to turn the hearts of parents to their children" (Luke 1:17 NRSV). The canonical implication is clear. John and the Jesus story to which he points are not new but are rather the next chapter in the narrative of God and God's people begun in the Old Testament.

Such continuity between the two Testaments is helpful for seeing how Jesus and his followers continue the story begun in the Old Testament. But this seamless story line should not obscure how jarring the transition actually is in turning from the Old Testament to the New. Indeed, many of the New Testament's most important words and concepts—"messiah," "**Sadducees**," "**Sanhedrin**," "synagogue," "crucifixion," and "resurrection," to name just a few—are rarely, if ever, even found in the Old Testament. Yet New Testament authors simply take for granted that their audiences will be as familiar with these topics as they are with David, Isaiah, and the Psalms. Why is this? Because the first-century world in which Jesus lived and the New Testament was composed was shaped not only by the history and theology recorded in the Old Testament but also by the tumultuous history of Israel between the Testaments.

What this suggests is that readers who want to understand the New Testament documents and the larger biblical narrative of which they are a part will need to pay some attention not only to the Old Testament canon but also to the centuries of intertestamental history, literature, and theology that sometimes get lost in the turn of the page from Matthew to Malachi.

The Story: Contribution to the Metanarrative

Israel's story in the intertestamental period begins where the plotline of the Old Testament left off: with Jerusalem under the authority of Persia. According to Ezra and Nehemiah, Persia defeated Israel's brutal captor, Babylon, and permitted the Jewish exiles to return home to rebuild both Jerusalem and God's temple. The remnant that returned to Jerusalem soon realized it was not the place it had been under Israel's great kings. The second temple paled in comparison to the one Solomon built, and the promised land on which it stood now belonged to the Persians. Many continued to wonder, as they had in exile, when God would fulfill the promises made to their ancestors. When would God restore the covenant and the kingdom? This question set the tone for God's people between the Testaments.

After two centuries under Persian rule, Israel found itself answering to **Alexander the Great**, the Greek conqueror who, in just over a decade, amassed an enormous empire that included the land of Israel. But Alexander's kingdom, one of the largest the world had ever seen, was short-lived. When the young king died in 323 BCE, his generals fought bitterly, eventually dividing Alexander's realm among themselves. Two of these generals, Ptolemy and Seleucus, spawned rival empires that successively controlled the land of Israel and thus significantly influenced the shape of Israel's faith and life in the time up to and including the New Testament.

Life under the Ptolemaic Empire (305–200 BCE) was relatively good for God's people, who lacked political independence but were largely granted religious autonomy. The high priest, the most powerful and sacred position within Judaism, generally oversaw religious and social affairs in Jerusalem, much as he had since the return from exile. Moreover, God's people under the Ptolemies were permitted to engage in the covenant-keeping practices integral to their identity as God's people: sacrificing at the temple, keeping Sabbath, and **circumcision**.

Any such religious tolerance disappeared, however, after Seleucus's empire won control of Israel from the Ptolemies (ca. 200 BCE). Hostilities between God's chosen people and their new overlords reached a boiling point when **Antiochus IV** ascended to the Seleucid throne. Antiochus's imperial policies struck at the heart of what was most sacred to devout Jews. He took control of the Jewish high priesthood, selling the hallowed position to someone loyal to him. When some Jews protested, Antiochus slaughtered thousands and ransacked the Jewish temple before ultimately banning the practice of Judaism on pain of death. Still more horrifying to many, Antiochus dedicated God's temple to the pagan god Zeus.

Anger among Jews turned to rebellion in 167 BCE, when one rural priest, Mattathias the Hasmonean, refused to participate in the pagan sacrifice Antiochus had mandated for Jews. Mattathias instead killed both an apostate Jew and a Seleucid official, fled to the mountains with his sons, and from there led other pious Jews in a guerrilla war of independence. Thus began the **Maccabean Revolt**, so named after Mattathias's eldest son, Judas Maccabeus (i.e., Judas "the Hammer"), who led the revolution following his father's death. Under Judas's leadership, the Jewish rebels eventually recaptured parts of Jerusalem (164 BCE), rededicating the temple to God and restoring the Jewish practices Antiochus had banned. The Jewish community still celebrates this improbable victory at the Festival of Lights, called "Hanukkah."

Leadership of the rebellion later passed to Judas's younger brothers, who retook control of the high priesthood and captured the Seleucid military fortress in Jerusalem, thereby securing both religious and political independence for the Jews. After centuries of subjugation to foreign powers—Babylon, Persia, Alexander, the Ptolemies, and the Seleucids—God's people were once again free to live and worship as God desired.

The Hasmonean family ruled over a free Israel for decades. Over time, however, they looked little different from the pagan rulers to whom Israel had for so long been subject. Their dynasty was characterized by naked political ambition, unseemly foreign alliances, and disregard for God's ritual laws. Infighting eventually culminated in a civil war between two Hasmonean brothers who fatefully turned to Rome—the rising superpower in the West—to help settle their rival claims to control the kingdom. In 63 BCE, the shrewd Roman general Pompey used this situation to take control of Jerusalem, thus bringing to an end a century of Jewish independence.

In 40 BCE, the Romans named **Herod the Great**—the Herod of whom we read at the beginning of Jesus's life—king over Israel.

Jewish regard for Herod was mixed. On the one hand, he tried to curry their favor by undertaking a massive renovation of the Jewish temple. On the other hand, many Jews resented Herod, not least because, as the Gospels rightly portray, his rule was marked by brutality and paranoia at the prospect of revived Jewish revolutionary zeal.

When Herod died after more than three decades in power, his kingdom was divided among his sons, who together compose the political backdrop against which the New Testament's story of Jesus unfolds. Herod Philip ruled over the area of Palestine north of Galilee. Herod Antipas ruled over Perea and Galilee, where Jesus spent his childhood and much of his ministry. This is the unpopular Herod that the Gospels mention in connection with both John the Baptist's execution and Jesus's trial. A third son, Archelaus, ruled over Samaria, Judea, and Idumea until the Romans replaced him with a procurator, a position most famously filled by the very Pontius Pilate who, at the behest of the Jewish leadership, ordered Jesus crucified.

The first-century Israel into which Jesus was born and in which the Gospel story unfolded was economically, politically, and socially very unstable. Like much of the empire, Jewish society was sharply divided between the poor masses and the powerful elites. Among the latter group was the Sanhedrin, an aristocratic council presided over by the high priest to which Rome entrusted some aspects of local government. Rome's notoriously repressive taxation, frequent meddling in sacred Jewish affairs, and heavy-handed suppression of any Jewish protest all contributed to a rising revolutionary fervor in Israel. While some only prayed for Israel's freedom, others, such as the **Zealots**, advocated armed resistance against their Roman occupiers. Indeed, by the time of Jesus's ministry, Israel had already seen several messianic pretenders—would-be deliverers of Israel—easily put down by Rome's military machine.

In 66 CE, the Romans set fire to the powder keg that was first-century Israel when they plundered the Jewish temple. The predictable Jewish protest was met with swift retribution. Much like the

Seleucids had done, the Romans killed thousands of protestors. Much like the Maccabees had done, Jewish revolutionaries led a revolt against their occupier. But this uprising ended far worse than the previous one. Four years of fighting resulted in the slaughter of tens of thousands and, most significantly, the destruction of the second temple. The intertestamental period thus had an all-too-familiar ending: no Jewish land, no Jewish kingdom, and no Jewish temple.

Two developments in this sweeping history from Ezra–Nehemiah to the Jewish Revolt are especially crucial for navigating the biblical story as it unfolds from the Old Testament to the New. The first is the tension that sometimes existed between Jews and non-Jews (i.e., "gentiles"), which can largely be traced back to Alexander the Great's policy of Hellenization, or exporting Greek culture to conquered lands. Because their sacred scriptures warned against mixing with foreigners and their gods, many Jews—more so than their non-Jewish neighbors—resisted adopting Greek language, philosophy, educational systems, religion, and so on. The issue became especially troubling under Antiochus IV, who harbored particular dislike for the Jewish religion. When he—and later, Rome—demanded the Jews' religious devotion, Hellenization became for many Jews not simply a matter of what language to speak but indeed a threat to the very survival of Jewish faith and life.

A second, closely related development critical for understanding the biblical metanarrative is the increasing diversity within Judaism in the time between the Testaments. This diversity arose partly in response to the question of **Hellenism**. We just said that many Jews rejected Greek culture. But there were nonetheless many others who, to varying degrees, happily embraced Hellenizing efforts. Diversity also developed over how and where to worship **Yahweh**. For some, the temple and the sacrifices made there under priestly leadership constituted the heart of proper worship. For other Jews—whether those living in the Jewish **dispersion** (or **Diaspora**) far from the temple or those simply disillusioned with corruption among priests who ran it—the temple's significance became increasingly symbolic. Rather than participate in temple practices, some groups, such as the **Essenes**, withdrew from society and sought to embody temple holiness in their community. For most Jews, religious and social life increasingly revolved around the synagogue, a newer, lay-run institution that in many ways is the precursor to the Christian church. This is where Jews would meet not to make sacrifices, as in the temple, but to read and debate about Torah, to pray, and to eat meals together.

By the time of the New Testament period, political and religious division within Judaism had more or less coalesced into three discernible groups, two of which are featured prominently in the New Testament. The **Pharisees**, who stand as Jesus's opponents throughout the Gospels, were a popular lay movement focused on the study and rigid application of the law—both the written Torah and the oral traditions of Torah interpretation—to all aspects of life. The Sadducees, whom the New Testament also pits against Jesus, were quite different from the Pharisees. Composed mostly of wealthy Jerusalem aristocrats, they were actively involved in temple worship and priestly leadership, held to a more conservative emphasis on only the written law, and tended to cooperate with the Romans more than other, less-privileged groups.

The Shape of the Story: Arrangement and Placement

The previous section argued for the importance of intertestamental history for understanding the dramatic social, political, and religious changes that took place between the conclusion of the Old Testament and the beginning of the New Testament. The obvious dilemma this poses in a book on the biblical metanarrative is that Alexander, Antiochus, and the Maccabees are never directly mentioned in the Bible that Protestants read. However, we do learn about these figures from a number of books Jews wrote in the intertestamental period, many of which are included in the canons read by millions of faithful Catholic and Orthodox Christians. Catholics refer to these books as **deuterocanonical**, from the Latin word meaning "secondary canon," and Orthodox communities call them *anagignōskomena*, from the Greek for "things that are read." Among Protestants, these texts are called **Apocrypha**, a word deriving from the Greek for "hidden things."

So what is the Apocrypha? Basically, it is a diverse collection of texts written by Jews during the intertestamental period. Together with other writings from the same period—such as Josephus's histories, the **Dead Sea Scrolls**, books ascribed to famous biblical figures such as Enoch, and the writings of Philo of Alexandria— these texts provide a window into the history and theology of the time between the Testaments. Some Christians tend to avoid the Apocrypha, assuming it is unnecessary to understanding the biblical metanarrative. But as we have already begun to see, these texts help to set the stage for the New Testament, and readers wanting to bridge the historical, literary, and theological gap between the Old Testament and the New would do well to learn something of them.

The Apocrypha's use and authority among early Christians is complex and somewhat obscure. On the one hand, it was the Christian community that preserved these texts, specifically as part of the widely used Greek translation of the Old Testament, the Septuagint. Furthermore, that several of the New Testament authors were familiar with the **apocryphal** writings is clear. The New Testament contains a handful of allusions to the Apocrypha and, as we will see below, some New Testament theology is indebted to some apocryphal texts. On the other hand, while New Testament authors frequently cite the Old Testament and other ancient Jewish texts (cf. *1 Enoch* in Jude 14), it is striking that they never directly quote the Apocrypha. Moreover, while the **church fathers** made regular, unambiguous use of the Apocrypha in the decades after the New Testament, it remains unclear precisely how much authority they gave these texts.

The status of the Apocrypha becomes somewhat more intelligible beginning in the fifth century, when Saint Jerome developed a new Latin translation of the Bible called the **Vulgate**. Because Jerome worked from the original Hebrew texts of the Old Testament and not from their Greek translations, the Vulgate was limited to those books found in the Hebrew canon of Scripture. The remaining texts—that is, the ones found in Greek versions of the Old Testament but not in the Hebrew Scriptures—he designated as "apocryphal," which is peculiar given that these texts were not actually "hidden things." What is clear from Jerome's designation, however, is that he took the apocryphal books to be qualitatively inferior to their Hebrew-only cousins and therefore unworthy to be included in the canon.

Jerome's opinion notwithstanding, the Western church later added the apocryphal books to the canon, where they remained without too much debate until the beginning of the Protestant Reformation in the sixteenth century. Martin Luther considered the Apocrypha "profitable and good to read" but denied it a place in the Bible because, among other reasons, the Catholic Church used these texts to support theological doctrines he found questionable. Important to notice, however, is that Luther did not remove the Apocrypha from his influential German translation of the Bible. Instead, he merely relegated it to its own, lesser place between the two Testaments. It is not until the nineteenth century that we find translations of the Protestant Bible produced without the Apocrypha, thus obscuring from view the valuable historical, theological, and literary value of these texts for understanding the biblical narrative.

The Style of the Story: Literary Features

Many first-time readers of the Apocrypha are surprised by how similar these texts can be to the Old Testament. Certain aspects are undeniably strange—for instance, Daniel's slaying of the dragon in the apocryphal story Bel and the Dragon. Nonetheless, much of what one finds in the Apocrypha will be familiar to readers of the Protestant canon. One finds, for example, books attributed to well-known biblical figures such as Manasseh, Baruch, and Jeremiah. One also finds in the Apocrypha many of the same literary genres found in the books of the Protestant Old Testament: theologically charged histories, such as 1–2 Maccabees (cf. 1–2 Samuel); edifying stories such as Judith and Tobit (cf. Esther); and Wisdom literature such as Wisdom of Solomon and Ecclesiasticus (cf. Proverbs and Ecclesiastes).

Aside from stylistic and literary similarities, the Apocrypha also deals with many of the same theological themes as the Old Testament. Among the many theological emphases found in both are God's faithfulness to the covenant, the close connection between God's glory and Israel's well-being, the importance of receiving and obeying the Torah, the temple as the preeminent place of God's glory, and the problem of suffering.

This is certainly not to say, however, that the Old Testament and Apocrypha are theologically identical or that the latter merely mimics the former. To the contrary, there are numerous instances of apocryphal books—as well as the broader collection of inter-testamental literature of which they are a part—taking up Old Testament themes and developing them in ways that later influenced New Testament authors. This is perhaps nowhere more striking than in the New Testament's teaching on the person and work of Christ.

To take one example, whereas Proverbs 9 famously personifies Lady Wisdom, the apocryphal book Wisdom of Solomon takes it a step further. Here, wisdom becomes "a reflection of eternal light, a spotless mirror of the working of God, and an image of his goodness" (Wis. 7:26 NRSV). It is this kind of intertestamental reflection upon God's eternality and goodness that then seems to provide the theological framework and language for New Testament authors seeking to articulate Jesus's relationship to God and creation. Thus Jesus is for Paul "the image of the invisible God, the firstborn of all creation" (Col. 1:15 NRSV) and, for the author of Hebrews, "the reflection of God's glory" (Heb. 1:3 NRSV).

A second example of this phenomenon is resurrection. Several passages in the Old Testament, particularly in the prophetic literature, speak of resurrection metaphorically—of Israel, for instance, returning from the "death" of exile. But only one Old Testament passage, Daniel 12:1–3, speaks of anything like a literal resurrection of the faithful who have died, a concept that of course informs virtually every page of the New Testament. So where did this concept develop? In the intertestamental period, particularly during Israel's persecution under Antiochus IV and his successors. One striking witness to this is seen in the book of 2 Maccabees, which tells the story of a mother encouraging her soon-to-be martyred son to resist Antiochus's torture and accept death "so that in God's mercy I may get you back again along with your brothers" (2 Macc. 7:29 NRSV).

We have focused here on the New Testament thinking about the person and work of Christ, but we could have easily focused instead on its understanding of God's perspective on the future, of angels and demons, or of the duality between body and soul, found throughout the New Testament. These are just a handful of the areas in which New Testament authors were influenced not only by the Old Testament but also by ways that intertestamental authors developed theological themes from the Old Testament.

The Specifics: What to Watch For

What Do We Learn about God?

Some people throughout history have characterized the time between the Testaments as a "silent period," the implication being that God ceased to speak in the centuries between the Old and New Testaments. But whether or not one believes God acted in the intertestamental period in the same way narrated from Genesis to Ezra–Nehemiah, or from Matthew to Revelation, there is plenty of evidence that God was at work in this period. Indeed, what we learn about God in the time between the Testaments is not essentially different from what we learn about God in the Old and New Testaments: that God will be faithful to promises made and will bless the world through Israel no matter their faults.

It may be helpful to think of the time between the Testaments as one of preparation for the Gospel story. As you read the literature and pay attention to the historical developments of the period, try to notice the ways in which God is preparing Israel and the world for what God will do in and through Jesus Christ. How is God preparing Israel for the arrival of their Messiah? How is God expanding Israel's theological imagination so that, under the Holy Spirit's guidance, they might one day make sense of Jesus's death and resurrection? And how is God preparing Israel to be a new kind of people, composed of Jews and gentiles alike?

What Do We Learn about Being God's People?

As God prepared God's people in the intertestamental period for the fulfillment of promises to come in Jesus, factions arose within Israel with competing ideas about how Jews might live faithfully in an increasingly antagonistic world. Pharisees attempted to apply the law to every detail of life, not because they were inherently judgmental but because they wanted their lives to glorify God. Others, such as the Essenes, fled from society not in order to escape the world but so that they might embody the temple's holiness standard when the temple no longer did. Still others embraced a revolutionary ideology, fighting for an independent Israel that might stand as a kingdom for Yahweh and his people in the midst of an unfaithful, idolatrous world.

But similar to both the Old and New Testaments, intertestamental history and literature demonstrate that for all their efforts, God's people seldom get it right. Single-minded focus on God's law manifests in legalism. Withdrawal from potentially corrupting influences easily becomes exclusivism. Fighting for God's kingdom on earth degenerates into nationalist pride, and those struggling for justice can quickly become the perpetrators of injustice. God's covenant people forget that covenant with God was never an end unto itself; God's desire had always been for a people through whom to bless the world.

As you read, look for ways in which Jews in the time between the Testaments, no less than in the Old Testament and the New Testament, struggle to be faithful to God and continually demonstrate the need for God's gracious intervention.

What Do We Learn about God's World?

First, we learn that the world was increasingly set against God's people in the intertestamental period. Whereas their Persian overlords had been content to let Israel worship Yahweh, the Greeks came to demand religious devotion in addition to land and taxes. Later, under the Romans, God's people were beset by rulers and neighbors hostile to them, their way of life, and their God. It is little wonder that for many Jews at the turn of the first century, the world could be divided into two kinds of people: Jews who worshiped the one true God, and gentiles and their sympathizers who did not.

Second, intertestamental history and literature reveal a world in desperate need of the one true King. Many kings came and went in the centuries between the Testaments. Some were benevolent, but most were not. Some had powerful kingdoms, others less powerful. Not all claimed divinity for themselves, but some did. Many, even if not all, were set against God's people. But not one of these proved to be the King who defends the cause of the poor and crushes the oppressor, the King whose glorious name endures forever and whose glory can fill the whole earth (Ps. 72). This is the one so many Jews waited for and thought about in the time between Malachi and Matthew.

When would God's kingdom finally come? When would God finally bless God's people and, through them, the world? Pay attention as you read to how these questions shape Israel's expectations in the time between the Testaments. And pay attention to how they can help us to understand the critical connection between the history and literature of these tumultuous centuries and the New Testament's witness to the life, death, and resurrection of the one true King, Jesus Christ.

8

The Story of Jesus

The Four Gospels

Laura C. S. Holmes

The Story: Contribution to the Metanarrative

The New Testament begins with four narratives of Jesus's birth, ministry, death, and resurrection called "Gospels," from the Greek word meaning "good news." On the surface, these four books tell the life of a Jewish man who did great deeds, taught love and judgment, died at the hands of authorities who disliked him, but was raised back to life by a God who loved him. Yet within the context of the biblical metanarrative, the Gospels contribute much more than such a simple story. Here we have nothing less than the climax of Scripture's metanarrative: Israel's Messiah has come!

The Gospels proclaim God's victory over evil and the renewal, restoration, and redemption of the world. They say that through

Jesus's life, death, and resurrection, humans see and experience the character of God more clearly than they ever had before. These texts—Matthew, Mark, Luke, and John—all bear witness to the moment God entered human experience most completely, by becoming one of us. Such a radical step enabled the restoration of humanity's relationship with God, with one another, and ultimately with creation itself. Jesus reveals the character of this God precisely because Jesus *is* God in flesh and blood. Jesus's life and death testify to a God who loves the world so much that God comes and ransoms the world that is trapped in evil, dying so that the insurmountable ties of sin and death could be vanquished.

The story of Jesus is the central part of God's story of renewing this world. As demonstrated by his resurrection, Jesus himself embodies the new life, or the kingdom, that God is bringing into the world. The Gospels proclaim that as a direct result of Jesus's death and resurrection, the Holy Spirit comes and continues the work that Jesus began. In other words, the Holy Spirit is teaching, comforting, and empowering disciples to bear witness to the "good news" until Jesus returns to complete his mission, finally and decisively saving the world.

The overall structure of the Gospel accounts is similar, yet they differ in details. For example, each Gospel describes Jesus's origin differently, but all of them have important connections to the Old Testament. For example:

Matthew: Jesus is a descendant of Abraham and David.

Mark: Jesus is the son of God, akin to the kings of Israel.

Luke: Jesus is born in an "impossible" way, like Hannah's "impossible" birth of Samuel (1 Sam. 1–2), but this time by a virgin.

John: Jesus is the divine "Word" that brought forth creation (Gen. 1).

In the next chapter of Jesus's life, the Gospels narrate how this "impossible" Son of God healed the sick, exorcised demons from the possessed, and taught about the **kingdom of God**—where God's will is done on earth as it is in heaven.

Not everyone responded well to Jesus. Some people did not like the way that this rabbi ("teacher") interpreted Israel's Scripture (i.e., the Old Testament). Others were not pleased with the crowds with whom Jesus chose to associate. Finally, still others were threatened by Jesus's claims that he was the Messiah, meaning one whom God has anointed in order to bring justice and deliverance to Israel and to the world. Being the Messiah was a threat, particularly to the Roman Empire's rule and those who benefited from the Roman Empire's support. As far as Caesar in Rome was concerned, there was only one ruler in the empire, and it was he.

Therefore, Jesus was crucified on a Roman cross, on the charge that he claimed to be the king of the Jews. Death by crucifixion was not just painful (a slow death by asphyxiation); it was shameful. Crosses were often placed along public roads into Jerusalem to serve as warnings to others who might rebel against Rome. However, Jesus's death wasn't just at the hands of Roman authorities; he was opposed by Jewish leaders, by crowds, by everyone. Even his disciples, those who had learned by his side ("disciple" means "learners"), would betray, deny, and desert him. Furthermore, the Gospels indicate that Jesus's death was also the result of Satan's activity; therefore, it has a cosmic dimension (e.g., Luke 4:13; 22:3). His death is not just about humans plotting against one another; it is also about God's victory over all forms of evil.

According to the Gospels and the testimony of the early church, God raised Jesus from the dead: the stone that enclosed him in the tomb was removed on the third day after his death, and several female disciples found the tomb empty. His disciples struggled to grasp the immense repercussions of this living Jesus's triumph over death. Jesus appeared to his disciples and promised that though he was leaving them to ascend to God, they would have the presence and power of God's Spirit in their lives together.

Just as God's Spirit had sent Jesus into the wilderness (e.g., Mark 1:12–13), so the Spirit of God would be empowering Jesus's followers as they spread the good news (gospel) he had given them. This gospel was that God's rule of righteousness and justice and grace—God's kingdom—had arrived in Jesus. Jesus signaled that he brought new life in his healings, exorcisms, and teaching. He demonstrated a way of love in sacrificing himself for others. And he conquered death itself by rising from the dead, never to die again. This is the beginning of the new life promised to believers both now and forever: this new life is one marked now by an abundant life of love and service that Jesus modeled. His disciples are to go tell and embody this news, just as Jesus did, in the power of the Holy Spirit.

The Shape of the Story: Arrangement and Placement

More than one account of Jesus's birth, ministry, death, and resurrection emerged fairly quickly. In fact, four of these accounts were used widely in congregations throughout the Roman world. When these Gospels were read in churches, they helped people live more in line with God's Spirit. Nevertheless, there were certainly some skeptics who criticized the church's use of these four accounts. The very fact that there were four narratives implied that one account was insufficient or, alternatively, that they were imperfect versions by themselves.

Significantly, readers noticed differences between these accounts. While the overall story is very similar (see the section above, "The Story: Contribution to the Metanarrative"), there are certainly variances in the way that the Gospel writers tell the story. For example, in the Gospel of Matthew, the "Christmas story" of Jesus's birth contains an angel's appearance to Joseph, a murderous and paranoid King Herod, and wise men who travel a great distance to worship Jesus. In the Gospel of Luke, however, we find the story of John the Baptist's birth, an angel's appearance to Mary, and lowly shepherds as Jesus's first visitors. There is no denying that these stories are very different.

From the beginning, there have been several responses to these kinds of differences. One path that the church might have taken would have been to select only one Gospel. One man, Marcion (85–160 CE), is known for trying this approach. He did not like the Old Testament very much, which makes reading the Gospels challenging: they are saturated with Old Testament quotations and allusions. Marcion liked only Paul's letters and some of the Gospel of Luke, so he created his own collection of texts to read by selecting those passages he liked and ignoring the others. While this certainly made reading the Gospels easier—there are no discrepancies when you have no other Gospel accounts to compare with Luke—the church chose not to go this easier way.

An early church leader named Tatian chose a different option: he combined all of the Gospel accounts. If we harmonize the stories of Matthew and Luke that are summarized above, we find infanticide, wise men, angels appearing to Mary *and* Joseph, and shepherds all in one compelling Christmas story. The problem is that this all-encompassing Christmas story is in none of the Gospels in its entirety. While Tatian's harmonization of the Gospels was popular in the Eastern church for a while, its influence was limited. Ultimately, the church decided not to read the Gospels as though they were one document: the church needed to be able to see both the similarities and the differences in the stories about Jesus.

Combining the Gospels into a bigger story, where their differences are harmonized, does not do justice to the church's affirmation that these *four* stories contribute greatly to our understanding of Jesus's identity and what it means to follow him. In the late second century, Irenaeus of Lyons attests to the church's usage of four individual Gospels, collected together. Irenaeus declares that there is room for diversity within the Gospels, but that they are unified by one Spirit. Each Gospel does not compete with the others, but they converge together to testify to the gospel, the good news of God's action in Jesus Christ. In other words, there are many ways to describe who Jesus was and is, but there are also some ways that are inappropriate and inaccurate. A four-Gospel canon provides both the space and the limits (or, to use another metaphor, the road and the guardrails) for following this Jesus.

What do we do with the "space," the differences, between the Gospels, then? Part of the task of reading the Gospels with the church is to look for the unique qualities of Jesus that each Gospel can provide. Sometimes these are different stories that serve a writer's overall purpose. In others, these are different approaches to the same story. At times the differences are minor; at times they can seem irreconcilable. *The point is to read the differences in light of the overarching purpose of the writer's portrait of Jesus* (see the last section below, "The Specifics: What to Watch For"). For example, Matthew's Gospel portrays Jesus as escaping from infanticide at the hands of a paranoid ruler and later traveling to and from Egypt because he portrays Jesus as a new Moses. This new Moses will teach Israel how to obey the law. Luke's Gospel has shepherds come to visit the infant Jesus because he will emphasize how Jesus has come in humility to deal with the grit and dirt of human existence. Jesus does not just come among the humble and poor ones of society, he delivers the least and the lowly.

The variations between the Gospels do not discredit them, because the purpose of each Gospel is not to state the facts about Jesus's life. Knowing the facts about people does not fully help us understand who they are; facts may sketch an image, but they do not complete a picture. We need to become familiar with the *way* people live their lives by spending time with them, listening to them, and watching them. Therefore, Jesus's disciples benefit from these stories about him because they add depth to their understanding of who Jesus is.

Furthermore, the Gospels teach us about the way Jesus *is still living*. This is the radical proclamation of the story of Jesus's resurrection. In this way, readers of the Gospels need to treat them not as compilations of a great individual's life but rather as four different, but indispensable, introductions to the living Jesus who is shaping their lives now. Accurate readings of the Gospels only begin with the text; they never end there. They are always to be lived out within the community of faith in the world.

Since we do have four Gospels, however, we can also ask one additional question. Why were they ordered in the canon Matthew, Mark, Luke, and John? For a variety of reasons, most interpreters believe that Mark's Gospel was written first, but it is not placed first. The order of the Gospels in the canon is not based on the order in which they were written; instead, it is based on the ways the Gospels help the church live out Jesus's call to discipleship.

Matthew makes sense as the first book in the New Testament canon in part because Matthew is so explicitly connected to the Old Testament. Matthew is saturated with Old Testament allusions, echoes, and citations in a much more obvious way than the other Gospels ("this was done to fulfill what had been spoken by the Lord through the prophet . . . ," e.g., Matt. 1:22–23). For example, Matthew connects directly to Malachi, the final book in the Old Testament prophets, which predicted the coming of Elijah (Mal. 4:5–6). Matthew introduces us to a new Elijah in Matthew 3, as John the Baptist (see Matt. 11:12–14) offers a baptism of repentance for the forgiveness of sins. Matthew begins with a genealogy that seems to echo much of the Old Testament, especially Genesis. Since this is the only Gospel to mention the "church" (16:18; 18:17), its steady recollection of the Old Testament reminds the reader that Israel's biblical story continues with Jesus and the church. Lastly, Matthew describes the journey of discipleship with remarkable clarity and confidence. There is little that is challenging about the *idea* of discipleship in Matthew; it is understandable. It is the *execution* of the idea, or the *doing* of discipleship, that is difficult.

Once we turn to Mark, however, things look different. While about 90 percent of the Gospel of Mark is included in the Gospel of Matthew, Mark has an entirely different feel to its narrative. This is due, in part, to Mark's illustration of discipleship. The disciples in Mark have a great deal of trouble understanding much of anything that Jesus says or does (e.g., Mark 4:13; 8:14–21). In Mark, being a disciple of Jesus is rife with uncertainty. Ignorance does not prevent the disciples from following Jesus, but it certainly unsettles Matthew's sense of clarity.

The Gospel of Luke suitably follows Matthew and Mark in part because all three have parallel narratives and stories. In fact, these Gospels are so similar that readers can put accounts from these three Gospels in columns and easily compare them. They are called "Synoptic" (*syn* = "together"; *optic* = "seen") Gospels for this reason. Luke portrays a balanced view of discipleship: it is difficult, it is confusing, but it is possible with God, who does the impossible. In light of this theological claim, Luke approaches discipleship from a different perspective. Luke's view of discipleship is concentrated on the object of discipleship: serving (and becoming) the least and the last in the world, whom God will impossibly make first (13:30).

The Gospel of John, however, is quite different from Matthew, Mark, and Luke. When read after these first three, it often seems to fill in the gaps of the others, clarifying and explaining events. While all the Gospels are engaged in interpreting Jesus's life as they tell the story of his ministry, John is more obvious about this process of interpretation.

It is John's ending that has cemented its role as the final Gospel. In this conclusion, John narrates the restoration and forgiveness of Peter, one of Jesus's central followers (John 21:15–19). The story of Peter's spiritual healing, found only here in the Gospels, looks forward to the book of Acts. There, after having been restored in the Gospel of John, Peter will be a primary actor in Acts' story of the church's beginnings.

In summary, Matthew introduces the Gospels clearly and well, with many connections from the Old Testament. Mark questions the clarity that Matthew illustrates in the life of a disciple, and claims that it is not always straightforward. Luke emphasizes those to whom Jesus preaches and ministers, the objects of discipleship: those who are "the least of these." Finally, John prepares the way for Acts, connecting Jesus's life and ministry to the story of God that began at creation and will continue until the **consummation** of the age.

The Style of the Story: Literary Features

In terms of style, the Gospels are clearly narratives. Therefore, skills acquired in English classes are helpful in reading them: consider their plot, their characters, their settings, and the way they describe time passing. All of these facets of the Gospels make them compelling stories. The early church found that it was not enough simply to say, as in a creed, that Jesus came, died, and rose again (e.g., Phil. 2:5–11; Col. 1:15–20). They needed to retell the story of Jesus's life. How did he interact with people? How did individuals respond to him? Retelling the story of Jesus reminds us of who he is, who we are, and how we should live.

The Gospels are not just narratives, however. They are narratives whose focus is primarily on one character. We generally call such accounts "biographies." However, the Gospels are far more like ancient biographies than modern biographies. For example, modern biographies often focus a great deal on the subject's childhood, which follows modern psychology's claims that we can explain a lot about an adult's life by examining his or her childhood. The ancient Mediterranean world, however, had no such interest in childhood stories of great individuals. Ancient biographies describe their birth, deeds, and death. Essentially, claiming that the Gospels are biographies simply means that their focus is on the adult life of Jesus as Messiah. It also explains why we do not know anything about Jesus's life as a teenager: ancient biographies did not cover this.

The point of the Gospels is to tell us what we need to know about Jesus in order to understand, believe, and follow him. The more we know about his identity, the better disciples we will be. Forming faithful, active, and loving disciples who bear witness to God's revelation in Jesus is precisely the purpose of the Gospels themselves (see John 20:30–31). Furthermore, the Gospels do not tell the story as though it is currently happening, like a videographer might. Instead, they tell the story of Jesus's life from a postresurrection perspective. The Gospels are not mystery novels: you're supposed to read them with the end (i.e., death and resurrection) in mind. Moreover, the writers of the Gospels were not striving to be neutral observers, even if that were possible. They were convinced that Jesus's life, death, and resurrection had made all the difference in the world. They wanted their readers to be convinced of this, too, so that readers would continue to follow Jesus in faith.

There are other genres within the Gospels as well. If you read Matthew, Mark, and Luke, you will find that Jesus frequently tells parables about the kingdom of God. A parable is a statement that compares something—often from nature—to the kingdom of God in order to illustrate what the kingdom is about or to point to who God is. Parables are rarely interpreted in a straightforward manner; in fact, the point of a parable is to make its hearers think hard about God, Jesus, and discipleship. We are in danger of totally missing the point if we assume that parables are easy to "get" (see Mark 4:10–12).

Furthermore, the Gospel writers often describe Jesus using irony and **hyperbole** in his teaching. Irony and hyperbole, like parables, are techniques to make the writer's audience question their assumptions and to think about how the kingdom of God is present in their lives, especially in Jesus. Recognizing the irony and hyperbole in the text is crucial for an accurate reading of the Gospels. Furthermore, familiarity with the Gospel story can cause interpretive blindness if the Gospels aren't read with attention to, and recognition of, these writing techniques and patterns.

The Specifics: What to Watch For

What Do We Learn about God?

In the Gospels, we learn first and foremost that God is revealed in Jesus Christ. The Gospels describe the relationship between God and Jesus in different ways. Nevertheless, the fundamental claim of the four Gospels is always the same: by his words and actions, Jesus discloses God's character and purpose to believers and to the whole world.

God is revealed in Jesus Christ in a more personal, close, and human way than the world had ever experienced before. It is not that the world—or God's chosen people, Israel—did not know God before. Israel had the Law and the Prophets. They had experienced God's deliverance from Egypt and from exile, and celebrated God's acts on their behalf. And at the same time, the Gospels proclaim that the way that God was embodied in Jesus was a completely new experience for Israel.

Remember: each Gospel describes God's revelation in Jesus in a slightly different way. Keeping these distinctive themes in mind often helps make sense of the differences in the details among the Gospels.

For example, Matthew describes God in Jesus Christ as a consummate teacher and interpreter of Scripture. Jesus interprets the law, just like Moses did; in fact, he interprets the same law that Moses did (Matt. 5). Many of the conflicts within Matthew are between Jesus and his contemporary interpreters of the Jewish law. Jesus is not giving a new law; instead, he is arguing with others (often Pharisees) about how to interpret the law that they share. Jesus is described both as a son of Israel and as the son of David, the fulfillment of God's covenants with Abraham and with David. And, finally, Matthew proclaims that Jesus's continuing presence will be with the community always, even when Jesus has left them to ascend to God (Matt. 28:20).

In Mark, there is a greater emphasis on Jesus's suffering. Jesus suffers, knowingly going to his death on a cross, precisely so that he can serve as a "ransom for many" (Mark 10:45). He gives his life like a servant or a slave, and yet he has the authority to command demons to leave those they have possessed (1:21–27) and to heal the sick (1:28–31). This portrayal of Jesus emphasizes his unpredictability: you can't nail this Jesus down and expect him to stay dead. He'll break out of the tomb and lead you on, somewhere else, just as he has said (16:7).

In Luke, we find that Jesus specializes in bearing others' burdens, in caring for those who have no power or ability to care for themselves, and in seeking out the ones society has forgotten for one reason or another (wealth, illness, status, race, gender, religion). Jesus is one who is known to forgive sins (7:36–50; 17:3–4) and to seek after those who are lost (15:1–32). He exhorts and empowers his disciples to do the same.

In John, Jesus reveals the character, nature, and actions of the Father. John describes Jesus as one who is both God (1:1, 14; 20:28) and Lord (20:28), indicating that this really is Yahweh, the God of Israel, in human flesh (the Synoptic Gospels affirm this claim too, but in more subtle ways). In John, Jesus often demonstrates a divine sense of foreknowledge of, and control over, his situation. For example, at Jesus's arrest, the guards only come to arrest him once he has finished speaking to his disciples (in contrast with the Synoptics) and he tells the guard to let them go, whereas his followers flee of their own fearful accord in the Synoptics. However, this very in-control Jesus is also very human in John. He weeps with Mary when her brother, Lazarus, is dead (11:35). He is tired and thirsty after a long day's travel (e.g., 4:6; cf. 19:28). The amazing claim of this Gospel is not that God is Spirit (4:24); it is that God has become flesh (1:14). And this fleshly Jesus is the one who can best teach us God's character.

What Do We Learn about Being God's People?

We can see God's care for people in all four Gospels. It is clear that God is involved with the world, with creation, and with humanity in particular, so much so that God became one of us. What we primarily learn about being God's people, however, is what it means to follow this Jesus who reveals God's nature and character so well. Christians are to bear witness to Jesus's work in our own lives, in the church, and in the world.

Again, different Gospels testify to diverse dimensions of what it means to follow Jesus. According to Matthew, for example, discipleship primarily focuses on the deeds that you do and ensuring that those deeds line up with the words that you say. A disconnect between what you say and what you do is classified as hypocrisy, the primary sin of the Pharisees in Matthew. Discipleship looks like the alignment of words (or thoughts) and actions. This is clearest in the Sermon on the Mount (Matt. 5–7), which is a succinct summary of the life of discipleship in Matthew. Following Jesus primarily focuses on the deeds that one does, not to gain Jesus's favor but to live out the grace and forgiveness that Jesus's presence offers. The community that Jesus builds, called the "church," is a place where sins are forgiven, where prayers are answered, and where life itself demolishes the power of death.

In Mark, Jesus unsettles our expectations about what he will do or where he will go. Mark's portrayal of the disciples is sometimes positive, as they do what Jesus has commanded (e.g., Mark 6:6b–13, 30–32), but more often than not, it is astonishingly negative: they do not understand at all, and, in some ways, they oppose Jesus and his ministry (8:14–21; 10:32–45). Nevertheless, Jesus continually calls his disciples to one action: death. This may indeed mean physical death, but it at least means a death of oneself, and one's selfish dreams and desires that may be in opposition to the coming kingdom of God. When one knows nothing else, one knows this: "Take up your cross, and follow me," Jesus says (8:34).

Luke proclaims that discipleship is seeking the kingdom of God wherever it may be found. In Luke, the kingdom of God is always found in unexpected places. To seek this kingdom, one must be prepared to offer, and receive, forgiveness. Following Jesus in Luke can involve challenging words to the rich and comforting words to the poor (e.g., Luke 6:20–26; 14:12–24; 18:18–25). It provides encouragement to seek the lost and forgotten, and it provides for deliverance for them when they are found (15:1–32). It involves embodying the actions of the Good **Samaritan**—the (often hated) outsider showing mercy and hospitality for a stranger (10:25–37). Following Jesus looks like imitating him, as the Holy Spirit enables disciples to do.

The Gospel of John describes discipleship in different terms, but in a way that complements the previous Gospels. When Jesus is speaking with his disciples before his arrest, he gives them a "new commandment," to love one another (John 13:34). In strictest terms, this is not a new commandment: the Old Testament commands Israel to love their neighbors (Lev. 19:18), and other disciples would surely be considered neighbors. The new aspect, however, is that the disciples are called to love one another as Jesus loves them. This means their love should look like Jesus's love does: washing feet, dying on a cross, and resurrecting from a tomb. Jesus does not mean this in a literal sense; most of his disciples would not become employed as servants, be crucified, or be resurrected in the way that he was. However, Jesus's self-sacrificial service and death are ways in which he exhibited love for his disciples, his friends. A further way was through his resurrection. Disciples are not only supposed to "die" sacrificially in love for one another, they are also to live sacrificially in such a way that ultimately brings life out of death. They are enabled to do this by remaining connected to Jesus through the power of the Holy Spirit (John 15:1–17).

What Do We Learn about God's World?

The most memorable thing we learn about God's world in the Gospel tradition is that God loves the world, and such love results in Jesus coming among us (John 3:16). God never gave up on the world or on Israel. The Gospels record positive and negative responses to this expression of God's love. However, the Gospel narratives do not allow their readers to divide the characters into "good" and "evil," as though God does not love everyone. Instead, the Gospels allow us to see how Jesus's disciples are fallible, and how they can even oppose Jesus's ministry, and yet God can work through them. They show how Jesus's enemies can be awful, but that they can also speak truth without knowing it. God loves the world—all of it and all in it.

Finally, the redemption that Jesus offers is not just about forgiving individuals their sins. It is about the redemption of all of creation. Jesus has come to repair not just humanity's relationship with God but also humanity's relationships with one another (hence, "love one another," even one's enemies) and with the rest of creation. There are reasons that the kingdom that Jesus is embodying is described with allusions to Genesis 1–2, especially in Matthew and John. The Gospel writers recognize that in Jesus, God embodies a new creation, precisely what God created humans to be. It is this new life to which Jesus and the Gospel writers call us to bear witness. The Gospels point to the time when all will acknowledge Jesus, whose death and resurrection lead us to the final, never-ending story, where Jesus comes again and creation is fully restored. The new life available now is only the beginning.

9

The Story of the Church

Acts and the Letters

David R. Nienhuis

The Story: Contribution to the Metanarrative

The story narrated in the Acts of the Apostles begins right where the Gospels left off—with the community of Jesus's disciples gathered one last time around their resurrected Lord to receive his final instructions. Jesus tells his followers to wait there in Jerusalem for the power of God to come down once again—this time in the person of the Holy Spirit, for through this Spirit God would empower them to be Jesus's "witnesses in Jerusalem, in all Judea and Samaria, and to the ends of the earth" (1:8 NRSV).

Soon thereafter the Spirit of God does indeed come down upon them to dwell within and among the people, empowering them to be God's restored Israel, the church (chap. 2). Filled with the Spirit, this community of Jewish believers in Jesus became immersed in the power of God so that they too would be able to do what their Lord did before them—that is, to proclaim the truth about God and to live together as newly restored humans in accordance with God's intentions for the world.

The early leaders of the church (called "apostles," from the Greek for "ones sent out") soon took this good news about God out beyond the boundaries of Israel, starting new church communities in every region (Acts 9–28). As they traveled about, they wrote letters of instruction and encouragement to the churches they formed, and these were eventually collected and distributed among all the churches (the twenty-one letters of Romans through Jude). Though the Christians were spread throughout the Mediterranean world and made up of many different types of people (Jews and Greeks, slaves and free persons, males and females—Gal. 3:28), all of them were unified by the Spirit as a new human community, a community whose words and deeds would make real the "new creation" God has planned for the whole earth.

The Shape of the Story: Arrangement and Placement

The section of the story surveyed in this chapter represents a huge amount of the biblical text. It makes up about half of the New Testament, encompassing twenty-two of its twenty-seven texts. Indeed, this story of the early church is given about as much "canon space" as the story of Jesus, which should tell us something about the nature of God's salvation: though the biblical story reached its climax in Jesus, it is in no way resolved there. God sent Jesus not only to die for our sins; he was sent to establish a community of disciples who would be empowered by the Spirit to spread his teaching and continue his work in the world until God's plan for creation might reach its conclusion.

No other New Testament book plays a more crucial canonical role in mediating this transition than the Acts of the Apostles. It is not uncommon for biblical scholars to describe Acts as a kind of "bridge text" that propels the biblical story forward as it transitions from the gospel of Jesus to the story of the church's ministry of the gospel for the sake of the world. Acts accomplishes this "bridge" function by enabling readers both to *look back to the Gospels* and also to *look forward to the letters*.

The manner in which Acts looks back to the Gospels is easily discernible. Simply put, in the Gospels Jesus calls believers to follow him, and in the Acts of the Apostles believers are shown following. In John's Gospel Jesus told his disciples, "Very truly, I tell you, the one who believes in me will also do the works that I do and, in fact, will do greater works than these, because I am going to the Father. *I will do* whatever you ask in *my name*, so that the Father may be glorified in the Son" (John 14:12–13 NRSV, emphasis added).

As you read Acts, notice how Jesus's "name" functions in the life of the believers: they teach in his name (e.g., 4:17–18; 5:28), they perform miracles in his name (e.g., 3:6, 16; 4:30), they cast out demons in his name (e.g., 16:18), and salvation and the forgiveness of sins are offered in his name (e.g., 4:12; 10:43). As the idea repeats throughout the book, the reader gets the clear sense that it is Jesus who is somehow continuing his own miraculous work in and through his apostles.

Of course, Jesus isn't there with them physically, and he doesn't somehow "possess" the apostles to force them to do his work. God sent Jesus in the flesh to be the New Adam, to provide a basis on which the newly restored humanity might emerge (Rom. 5:15–19; 1 Cor. 15:21–22). When the Spirit is breathed into these believers (John 20:21; recall Gen. 2:7) they are transformed over time in order to become mediators of the real presence of Christ in the world.

This transfer is made explicitly clear when we see the apostles replicating Jesus's famous deeds. Just as the Spirit descended on Jesus while he was praying after being baptized (Luke 3:21), so also the believers are baptized by the Spirit while they are praying (Acts 1:14; 2:1–4). Just as Jesus heals a lame man early in his ministry (Matt. 9:2–8 and parallels), so also Peter does the same early in

Acts (Acts 3:1–10). Just as it is enough to touch Jesus's cloak to be healed (Matt. 9:20–21 and parallels), so also those who touch articles of clothing touched by Paul receive healing (Acts 19:11–12). Just as religious and political leaders persecute Jesus, so also those same people persecute the believers (e.g., Acts 4:1–22; 5:17–42). Just as Jesus, dying on the cross, says, "Father, forgive them; for they do not know what they are doing," and at his death, says, "Father, into your hands I commend my spirit" (Luke 23:34, 46 NRSV), so also Stephen, dying under a hail of stones, says, "Lord Jesus, receive my spirit" and "Lord, do not hold this sin against them" (Acts 7:59–60 NRSV).

So the Acts of the Apostles is obviously intended to show that the salvation wrought by Jesus in the Gospels is continued in and through the work of the church. But then how does Acts prepare the reader to receive the apostolic letters that follow? It is striking to note that though Acts seems to have been written by the same person who wrote the Gospel according to Luke, a study of the church's reception of biblical books shows that while Luke became part of the fourfold Gospel collection rather early on, its companion volume languished in disuse. Only later when it was taken up to function as the required introduction to the New Testament letters did it find its true function. Accordingly, the final placement of Acts is *not* alongside Luke as a two-part work from a single author but after John and before the first apostolic letter. This suggests that introducing the New Testament letters is the book's more crucial role. But how does it function in this regard?

Several points can be made. *First, Acts provides biographical portraits of the letters' authors.* Gospel readers might not be confused when they come upon the letters of Peter and John, but can you imagine finishing John's Gospel and turning the page to read Romans? You'd be completely confused, wondering, "Who is this Paul guy?" Acts alleviates the confusion; before we ever start reading Paul's letters we know that he is a Pharisee and former persecutor of Christians who was called by Messiah Jesus to preach God's gospel to both the Jewish and non-Jewish world.

We know that Paul proclaimed Jesus to the whole northwestern Mediterranean world, that he was persecuted, arrested multiple times, and put on trial before governors and kings because of his work for the gospel. And just as Acts ends with Paul preaching the gospel in Rome (Acts 28:23–31), we then turn the page and find Paul's Letter to the Romans—and the transition from Gospel to Paul is made smoothly.

Though he plainly can't be said to play a prominent role in Acts, the narrative's introduction of James the Lord's brother is of crucial importance for our understanding of the New Testament as a whole. Quite a number of people named James are mentioned in the Gospels, the most important of them being James the brother of John. That particular James is executed by Herod at the beginning of the twelfth chapter of Acts. At the end of that chapter, when Peter is miraculously delivered from prison, he instructs his surprised comrades to "tell this to James and to the believers" (12:17 NRSV). Which James is he talking about?

Reading on, we find that this James is the leader of the church in Jerusalem; he provides the concluding judgment at the apostolic council (15:13–21), and he receives reports from Paul and is able to command him to do his bidding (21:17–26). Whoever this James is, he's apparently a very powerful and important early Christian leader! Turning from there to the letters of Paul, we find the mystery is resolved: this is James the Lord's brother (Gal. 1:19; cf. Matt. 13:55; Mark 6:3), the one who received a direct resurrection appearance from Jesus (1 Cor. 15:7) and was subsequently named the first of three "pillars" of the Jerusalem church (Gal. 2:9). Once we recall the Acts narrative where we are told that Jesus's brothers were present along with the disciples in Jerusalem at Pentecost (Acts 1:14), the mystery is solved: this is James, the Lord's brother, the first head pastor of First Church Jerusalem. By the time we finally reach the Letter of James, we understand why the author is able to command his readers to action with such authority!

A second way Acts introduces the letters is similar to the first: *Acts provides a narrative context within which our reading of the letters is rightly "framed."* If we didn't have Acts to function as a kind of map, we'd struggle to figure out precisely how the letters fit on the landscape of early Christianity. In this regard, Acts doesn't simply continue the story of Peter and John and introduce us to new people like Paul and James. It also introduces us to places like Ephesus, Philippi, Ethiopia, and Rome. It introduces us to ideas like missionary journeys and church plants. It reminds us that earliest Christianity wasn't directly tied to one person, one place, one ethnic group, or one gender. Indeed, Acts reminds us that earliest Christianity was *catholic*—from a Greek word meaning both "universal" and "whole." It had no one cultural "home" and did not belong exclusively to any one ethnic group. It was mediated by well-known leaders like Peter and Paul as well as those lesser known (like Philip, Stephen, Lydia, Priscilla and Aquila, and Apollos) and even those who remain completely unknown to us. The Christian church is a community of diverse believers, from diverse places, with a diverse set of concerns. That same diversity is reflected in the twenty-one letters that follow.

In this regard, *Acts helps us to understand that the earliest Christian mission was "two-sided."* It began with a mission headed by Jewish believers (especially Peter and John) and directed toward Jewish people in and around Jerusalem (Acts 1–7). Before long, that Jewish mission began converting non-Jews to Christianity (Acts 10:1–48), and soon it commissioned a second mission directed to gentiles, the most well-known figure of which is Paul (Acts 15–28). As we turn to the letters, we find that the shape of the letter collection reflects this two-sided mission: the first fourteen letters are associated with the mission of Paul to the gentiles (Romans through Hebrews), and the next seven are associated with the leaders of the Jewish mission to Jews (the letters of James, Peter, John, and Jude). Note that the order, excluding the name of Jude, reflects Paul's ordering of those he calls "pillars" of Jerusalem in Galatians 2:9. When the Letter of Jude identifies its author as "Jude . . . brother of James" (Jude 1), we recall that Jesus had one brother named James and another named Jude (Matt. 13:55; Mark 6:3); the order of the letters implies that this final "Jerusalem pillars" collection (traditionally called the "Catholic Epistles") is meant to be received as though it was handed down to us in the "embrace" of Jesus's earthly family.

Finally, though by no means least important, is the fact that *Acts provides a narrative introduction to the issues and conflicts reflected in the letters.* For instance, Acts tells the story of a Christian church that originates within Judaism but ends up becoming made up primarily of gentile believers. Many of the New Testament letters (most especially those of Paul) struggle with the question of how a predominantly gentile church is to keep faith with the God of Israel revealed to the world in the Jewish Scriptures and principally in the Jewish Messiah, Jesus. After all, Jesus insisted his mission was directed to Israel (Matt. 15:24) and insisted that "salvation is from the Jews" (John 4:22 NRSV); and Paul maintains the priority of Israel by repeatedly insisting that salvation is offered "to the Jew first and also to the Greek" (Rom. 1:16 NRSV; cf. 2:9–10; 3:9; 10:12). Acts therefore maintains this same salvation logic: Christianity begins in a Jewish mission (Acts 1–7), which in turn gives birth to a gentile mission (Acts 8–28).

Another example: the Acts of the Apostles makes it perfectly plain that the Holy Spirit was bestowed on both men and women alike. Gender relations were closely policed in the ancient world, where women were viewed as the property of their eldest male relative and were not allowed to act as free agents or to take positions of authority over men. But in the Acts of the Apostles women are present right alongside the male disciples when the Spirit is poured out (1:14), and all of them begin to prophesy (2:14–18). Women are described as taking on the faith and leading their households independently of male counterparts (16:14–15, 40). They hosted house churches and engaged in ministry right alongside men (see, e.g., Rom. 16). In the case of one of the only couples named in Acts, the wife Priscilla is named *before* her husband, Aquila, more often than he is before her (18:2, 18, 26)—an act that went completely against the conventions of the time. Consequently, the letters describe both the wonders and the struggles of living and worshiping in a community where women and men are treated equally as co-heirs with Christ (see, e.g., 1 Cor. 11:3–16).

A final example may be found in the conflict over Paul, whose preaching was as much a challenge then as it is now. Paul's immense New Testament witness is as brilliant and stimulating as it is thought provoking and occasionally perplexing. Even in Paul's own day, many misunderstood what he was trying to say. Some thought he was preaching an obedience-free gospel: since we are made right with God entirely by grace, why should we obey God's commands (Rom. 3:8; cf. 6:1, 15)? Others, both friends and foes, thought Paul had rejected his Jewish past (Acts 21:20–21) since he sometimes drew a polarized distinction between God's law and gospel in a way that seemed to suggest, they claimed, that Christ had completely abolished the need for the law (Eph. 2:15; cf. Matt. 5:17–18). Some even thought Paul was the only real, true apostle of Christ (see, e.g., 1 Cor. 1:12–13, and also the second-century Christian heretic Marcion, who rejected both the Old Testament and the other apostles).

The final shape of the apostolic Acts and letters can be seen to offer a correction to these potential misunderstandings of Paul's message. His writings are introduced by the Acts of the Apostles, where Christianity is unapologetically rooted in Judaism and Paul is described as a leader among leaders. On the other side of the Pauline collection are the Catholic Epistles, where leaders of the Jewish mission offer their unique portrait of the gospel, and some of them even offer correctives to potential misunderstandings of the Pauline message (2 Pet. 3:15–17)—especially any misunderstanding that salvation could come "by faith alone" apart from an authentic and active life of discipleship (e.g., James 2:14–26; 2 Pet. 1:5–11). Thus, the New Testament presents Paul surrounded by his apostolic colleagues as a way of protecting against the sort of misunderstandings that arise when Christians receive their understanding of the gospel from Paul alone.

The Style of the Story: Literary Features

There are two primary literary forms at work in this section of Scripture: narrative and epistolary. Why are these two forms in particular given so much space in the New Testament? Why not some of the other genres we've encountered in the Bible? Why not a book entirely devoted to Christian poetry or hymns? Why not wisdom texts? Why not a single book of clear instructions on doctrine and worship? None of us can offer a definitive answer to this question, but we can describe the effect such a story and letter-heavy New Testament has on our understanding of Christian life and faith.

Stories, we might say, help us to "keep it real." Stories don't allow us to locate Christianity at a safe distance, lost somewhere in the clouds of abstract thought. In stories we meet real people, real characters, with real struggles and joys and failings and pains. We follow them as they walk the life of faith, and along the way we are provided glimpses of how Christianity is embodied and practiced in the real world. We are reminded that the Christian faith is a profoundly *human* faith, one that is not at all interested in somehow denying the flesh-and-blood realities of daily life. Christian faith is *practiced* by people; it takes its distinctive shape and tone according to the context in which it has materialized. Like our God, who refuses to stay apart from us in the purity of heaven but comes down to enter the world in concrete ways, so also Christian faith is "made flesh" in the people who live it out.

But what about the apostolic letters, which themselves make up nearly 40 percent of the New Testament? Before we describe what a letter-heavy New Testament communicates about Christian life and faith, a few technical comments are in order. As we noted earlier, the New Testament contains two letter collections. One group of letters comes from the apostle Paul and offers witness to the mission to the gentiles. The other group of letters, traditionally called the "Catholic Epistles," comes from apostles who knew Jesus in the flesh and were associated with the mission to Jews centered in Jerusalem. The distinction between the two collections is underscored in their titles: Paul's letters are titled "To the [recipients]," while the Catholic Epistles are titled "The Letter of [the author]." Though the Letter to the Hebrews is technically anonymous, many in the early church believed it to have been authored by Paul (hence the title "*To the* Hebrews"), so it is included as a kind of "appendix" to the Pauline collection.

Some of the New Testament letters are formal encyclicals written from a leader in order to be distributed to all Christians everywhere (e.g., James, 2 Peter, Jude). Others seem more like sermons that were ultimately distributed in letter form (e.g., Hebrews, 1 Peter, 1 John). Most of the letters, however, are what we might call "actual letters"—that is, letters that were written from one person or party to another.

These letters were written according to the genre expectations of the day and therefore follow a predictable four-part format. They begin with a two-part "letter opening." A **prescript** comes first, identifying the sender and recipient and concluding with a greeting (see, e.g., Phil. 1:1–2). A **proem** follows, which is a kind of warmhearted preface designed to ensure a positive reception for the letter. Proems typically include thanksgivings, prayers, and health wishes, as well as hints regarding the primary content of the letter (see Phil. 1:3–11). These elements set the stage for the third part, the "letter body," which will make up the bulk of the letter's content (the body of Philippians begins at 1:12). It can sometimes be difficult to determine precisely where the body ends and the fourth part, the "letter closing," begins, but typically we look for closing exhortations, references to the act of writing itself, and nitty-gritty topics like money and travel plans (notice how Phil. 4:8–9 seems to offer a conclusion, while 4:10 turns to the topic of financial support). The letter closing wraps up with a set of "farewell greetings"—the author sends along greetings to associates of the recipients, and then associates of the author send their greetings as well (Phil. 4:21–22). The letters then typically conclude with a farewell that often takes the form of a **benediction** (4:23).

The impressive weight of the letter genre in the New Testament tells us several important things about the nature of Christianity. First and foremost, we must say that the letters emphasize the essentially *communal* and *relational* nature of Christian faith. All of them are letters to churches or to leaders of churches. Nowhere do we find individual Christians pursuing an otherworldly "spiritual life" in isolation from others. These letters make it clear that where the Spirit is at work, people are able to live together in peace and harmony as a testimony to God's plan for the whole world (e.g., 1 Cor. 3:1–4; 12:27–13:13; Gal. 5:16–26; James 3:13–18).

Of course, the letters also make it plain that Christianity is essentially *missional*. When Jesus sent his disciples out into the world to proclaim the good news of God's kingdom, they did not do so by publishing books and articles on the subject. Jesus said, "Go therefore and make disciples of all nations, baptizing them in the name of the Father and of the Son and of the Holy Spirit, and teaching them to obey everything that I have commanded you" (Matt. 28:19–20 NRSV). So that's what they did! They prepared leaders and started churches, and those churches prepared more leaders who started more churches, and so the story goes on still today. This is the "job" Christ gave us, to create faith-forming communities of believers around the world that would follow the pattern established before them in order to be filled with the Spirit and transformed by the power of God's love.

Finally, we must note again how the letters remind us that Christianity is thoroughly *contextual*. While all Christians everywhere share a tradition of practice and belief, those practices and beliefs are embodied differently in the many different places they are "made flesh." For this reason, when we read the letters we encounter a Word of God landing very much "on target" in a particular time and place. Of course, those very specific, "targeted" texts were eventually taken up by the Spirit and canonized as applicable to all Christians everywhere, so we mustn't overplay the limits original context places on texts. Regardless, the letters witness to the fact that Christianity isn't a uniform, one-size-fits-all religion. When we read the letters, therefore, we should expect to find a good deal of diversity in the admonitions and exhortations given.

One final point must be added before we conclude this section on the literary features of the apostolic Acts and letters. The biblical story began with the creation of all things. It then told the story of Israel, then that of Jesus, and now the beginnings of the Christian church. The next book, the Revelation to John, leaps forward in time to provide us with a poetic glimpse of how the story of God's redemption ends. The Bible can therefore be said to be an "unfinished drama"; the story of the church is started, but we only hear about the earliest generations of Christians. The resulting historical gap within the Bible's story is meant to be filled out by all of us. As we work our way through the stories of Israel and Jesus and the earliest church, we are provided with a rich set of characterizations of the life of faith so that we may ourselves take up our appointed role as characters in the story of God's salvation. The Bible describes what came before, and how the story will end. What happens in between is God's work in and through the church in history, and that includes us.

The Specifics: What to Watch For

What Do We Learn about God?

So much could be said here! For now we'll content ourselves with the following claims. First, the apostolic Acts and letters seek to make it absolutely clear that *the Christian God is the God of Israel*. Notice how in Acts the apostles proclaim the gospel as the fulfillment of Israel's Scripture (e.g., 2:16–21; 3:18; 15:15–17; 28:25–28). What has taken place in Christ, they insist, was "necessary" in order to fulfill God's plan (1:22; 9:6, 16; 13:46; 14:22; 17:3; 19:21; 23:11; 25:10; 27:24). Christian faith did not emerge *in spite of* Jewish faith; it emerged *out of* Jewish faith and completes it. The corollary to this, of course, is the conviction that *the Scriptures of*

Israel are Christian Scriptures. Indeed, they are the indispensable guide to a right understanding of what God has done in Christ. As you read Acts and the letters, watch how the apostles strive to make clear that what has taken place in and through Jesus and the Holy Spirit is completely consonant with God's plan revealed in the people and Scriptures of Israel.

Because of this, Acts and the letters consistently describe the experience of God in what will eventually come to be called "trinitarian" terms. Jesus is the Messiah and Son of Israel's God, whose faithful death and glorious resurrection reveals God's faithfulness to humanity and establishes Jesus as King and Lord of all. Likewise, the Spirit was well known to Israel, and the Spirit's outpouring to empower believers for witness was long ago foretold by Israel's prophets. Christians have therefore been adopted by God to live in obedience to Christ by the indwelling power of the Holy Spirit. As you read, watch for this persistent "threefold" description of God's being and activity.

What Do We Learn about Being God's People?

Much has of course already been said in this regard, so for now we'll continue the trinitarian theme by describing its implications for the identity of God's people. First, as you read Acts and the letters it will become plain to you that a clear separation between religions called "Judaism" and "Christianity" is entirely unheard of in the New Testament. Christianity emerges as a sect of Judaism, all the earliest apostles were Jews, and for all of them, the only "Bible" they possessed was Israel's Scriptures. Christian believers therefore understand their identity and calling in terms of the redemptive work God started in and through the people of Israel. By extension, heresy and distortion have always occurred whenever Christians have tried to know Christ apart from the Old Testament. As the ancient church fathers liked to remind us, the Word by which the world was made is the same Word by which it is being redeemed. Creation and redemption, Old Testament and

New Testament, must be held together or the essential structure of Christian faith and belief falls apart.

Among the distortions that occur when creation and redemption are severed is the failure to understand the full implications of the apostolic proclamation that Jesus is Lord. Christian redemption does not save us *from* the world; it saves us *for the sake of* the world. As Acts and the letters make plain, Christian salvation is a vocation, an enlistment into the redemption project God has been working out since the time of Abraham and Sarah. Those who live "in Christ" therefore live within the realm of his grace-filled sovereignty and accept no other "lord" over their lives. By word and deed they take up his "cross-shaped," self-sacrificial model of life as the only right expression of trust in God and love toward others. In doing so, they participate in God's work of bringing reconciliation to the world.

All this takes place by the power of the Holy Spirit, who lives in and among Christians to cleanse them of their sin, enabling them to "put off" their old, selfish selves and "put on" the character of Christ. The apostles repeatedly insist that the Spirit is actively working to break down psychological and societal barriers of hostility that hold the world back from taking up its appointed reconciliation in Christ. As you read, watch for the myriad descriptions of how the three persons of the Trinity operate together to form a whole Christian life.

What Do We Learn about God's World?

Principally, we learn that the world is the creation of a faithful Creator who loves it and is actively working even now to reconcile all things. This process of restoring creation is taking place from the inside out, through the children of God whose transformed lives represent the "firstfruits" of the redemption that will one day be a reality for the whole creation. As you read, pay attention to how the apostles call us to inhabit a "resurrection imagination," one that sees the world and all that is in it not as something unclean or irredeemable, but as a reality filled with God's redemptive potential.

10

The Story's Conclusion

The Revelation to John

Eugene E. Lemcio

The Story: Contribution to the Metanarrative

Throughout its history, Revelation has been interpreted in ways that have produced controversy and frustration among intelligent and sincere readers both Christian and not. Readers are sometimes confused by the misinformed claims of those who assert theirs is the one and only correct view. In truth, no other biblical book enjoys such a range of interpretation. Most modern scholars read Revelation as a book written for early Christians who needed help to engage and endure the mighty Roman Empire at the end of the first century. Many popular television evangelists, on the other hand, pronounce that Revelation is a blueprint of all that will happen in their own lifetime. It is important, therefore, to consult a variety of recent commentaries on Revelation to get a good feel for the different approaches to the book's literary style and theological understanding.

It's especially important to consider the placement of Revelation within Scripture. As the final chapter in the metanarrative, this book logically tells how the biblical story of God's salvation ends. But "the end" in Revelation's case does not refer to creation's termination but to its purpose or goal, as in the expression "to what end?" The last chapters of this story are set not in heaven but on a new earth (Rev. 21–22). They show that all that had earlier opposed God's good purposes for humankind and the world has been removed to be replaced by the never-ending presence of God and Jesus. God has enabled John to prophesy. This means literally "to speak on behalf of" God. He is enabled to "uncover" (*apokalyptein* in Greek) the meaning of both the present—"what is"—and future—"that which is to come" (1:19). The author helps readers to interpret the here and now as well as to expect the there and then.

To accomplish this, John reaches back to earlier episodes in the biblical story. Two visions in the heart of Revelation illustrate the point. In chapter 11, there is a blending of three well-known series of pairs from the beginning, middle, and latter part of Israel's story: the priestly brothers Moses and Aaron (Exodus–Deuteronomy); the prophetic partners Elijah and Elisha (1 Kings 17–2 Kings 13); and the political-priestly figures Zerubbabel and Joshua (Zech. 3–4). Each figure in the set is a historical type or sign of the two witnesses to come in the last days. Their death and coming back to life show both the cost and reward of their faithfulness. The author's vision of chapter 12 extends the scale even further. In the past, anti-God activity was described almost entirely in human terms. However, John identifies the supernatural spirit behind it all: the devil, Satan, the dragon, that old serpent. Opposing forces range across both heaven/sky and earth—the entire cosmos being the battlefield. Whereas in the past the overcoming of enemies was accomplished by the use of conventional methods, such as power plays and military might, the most important battle in the entire biblical story is won by the sacrificial death of a vulnerable agent, symbolized as a lamb (12:11).

The Shape of the Story: Arrangement and Placement

Directly prior to Revelation there appear two sets of letters: those written by Paul (mainly to non-Jewish Christians) and those authored by the leaders of the mother church in Jerusalem, each representing a wing of early Christianity. Revelation adds another collection of letters to the New Testament, thereby providing a formal link to what comes before: chapters 2–3 are letters addressed to the seven churches of Asia (a Roman province in what is now western Turkey). Heading the list is the congregation at Ephesus, the capital of this province—a world-class city, politically and economically equivalent to New York City. It is very prominent in Acts 19 and the only one of the seven churches literarily represented in the rest of the New Testament. In fact, several New Testament books were written to or from Ephesus. And yet the message from the Spirit is to be heard by all of the churches, according to the ending of each letter. So far as the rest of the New Testament is concerned, Revelation is linked to the Gospels by way of "the little **apocalypse**" (Mark 13//Matt. 10 and 24//Luke 21). In them, Jesus looks to the future in much the same manner and with some of the same categories as John did. Finally, the book of Daniel, the single Old Testament document most like Revelation, contributes the following major categories to it and the first three Gospels: the kingdom of God and the Son of Man, Jesus's preferred means of self-identification, which appears at the beginning (chap. 1) and near the middle (chap. 14) of Revelation.

The Style of the Story: Literary Features

At the outset (1:1), John tells us that he received his revelation from God through signs, an important clue that modern translations do not usually convey. In other words, the message will be coming at readers indirectly rather than directly. They will be shown a series of visions loaded with symbols—probably his most distinctive indirect means of communication. However, this means of conveying truth is much undervalued within and outside of the church, as evidenced by the common expression "merely symbolic." They are often seen as the poor alternatives to "literal" or "objective." Yet symbols are powerful means of communicating, especially evident when they are abused or defaced—as in the case of flag burning. Such violent treatment causes a flare-up of thoughts, emotions, and action. Head, heart, and feet are all simultaneously affected. Word symbols, as well as object symbols, can produce a similar effect. When used as a form of communication, they can be even more powerful than narrative prose. Of course, the challenge is always to avoid treating the literal symbolically and the symbolic literally. Sometimes it's obvious. Is Jesus, as depicted in chapter 5, really a lamb? No, but he did sacrifice himself. Does he actually have seven eyes and seven horns? No, but he is all-seeing and all-powerful.

Sometimes the symbols will be used to create a sense of irony—the joining of opposites to create a contradiction or paradox for use in a constructive way. The goal is to disorient our common conceptions and practices in order to reorient them into a different way of thinking and acting. In some cases, numbers are employed as symbols—a phenomenon that occurs in many cultures. It's common for "one" to stand for the highest achievement. John's use of "seven" represents perfection or completeness. One encounters numerous sets of seven: seven churches, seven seals, seven trumpets, seven bowls, and so on. Each of the latter three sets of seven ends in a finale, leading the reader to wonder after each one, "How many times can a story end? What more could possibly happen afterward?" And the beginning of Revelation's contribution to the overall story (about a woman and her newborn son) starts at chapter 12! This should caution readers about treating this book as a chronological account from the beginning of chapter 1 to the end of chapter 22.

Furthermore, repetition should not necessarily be regarded as sequential. It may be a function of recapitulation, or the recapping of certain themes thought vital by the author. Or we might regard each as a facet of the whole—of a single jewel whose surfaces are being examined from various angles of vision. Biologists might find it useful to think of each set of seven as a twist of the microscope dial—each time seeing the stable, single specimen in greater detail. However, one should not rule out the possibilities of progress and intensification.

Even though John has not chosen chronological sequence to write down the visions he receives, there is an order to it, but of a different kind: literary rather than linear. For example, he arranges some of his visions according to a reversal technique. The most extensive example covers almost the entire second half of the book: (chap. 12) Dragon [A], (chap. 13) Beasts [B], (chap. 17) Babylon [C]—their Rise; (chap. 18) Babylon [C'], (chap. 19) Beasts [B'], (chap. 20) Dragon [A']—their Demise. This pattern of ABCC'B'A' is called "inverse parallelism." Such a switch can occur in smaller units, too. So not everything between chapters 12 and 22 needs to happen historically as written—or as "predicted."

The Specifics: What to Watch For

How should the dominant themes of this book be determined in a way that avoids the individualist trap of "my personal belief about Revelation is . . ."? A positive answer follows in the next section. But readers should also pay attention to what is *not* said or how a particular scheme does *not* occur. For example, the term "rapture," or the snatching away/up of believers, never appears in Revelation—or anywhere else in Scripture, for that matter. However, this fact hasn't stopped many self-identified Bible believers taking for granted that it does. Sometimes, this comes from relying too heavily on the opinions of various authorities. Furthermore, there is nothing in Revelation that speaks of Christians being taken up from earth to heaven. The term "antichrist" is never used in Revelation for the anti-God figure(s). We have to go to 1 John 2:18–19, 22–23 and 2 John 7 for this expression. There we read that *many* antichrists had *already* emerged from the Christian community during the first Christian century. In addition, vast numbers of believers have been taught that seven years of tribulation will immediately precede the millennium—a thousand-year period at history's conclusion. However, never is the number seven assigned to the great tribulation, which John cites only once (7:14). There, according to the Greek, it is continuously occurring; and never is it immediately followed by the one thousand years. In fact, the latter is mentioned only four times in the entire Bible—all in 20:2–5. About the number one thousand, many interpreters ask, "In a book so full of symbols, why take this number literally?" Therefore, one must be on the lookout for all rigid schemes and interpretations, especially those that are imposed from outside of the text rather than found within it.

What Do We Learn about God?

In Revelation, perhaps the dominant image for God is that of King. The reader finds an astonishing number of references to "kingdom," "authority," "power," and "throne"—all political categories. "Political" refers to the root meaning of the Greek word *polis*: "city." *Politics* is the art or strategy enabling the collective and individual good to flourish. Political science is the study of strategies that humans have invented to analyze the various options. Of course, the larger and more diverse the community, such as an urban center, the greater the challenge. According to Scripture, the best of such human schemes falls far short of what might be called the "politics of God"—that is, God's concern to address *first and foremost* the needs of those without power and prestige. This point is dramatically illustrated by the fact that the main salvation event of the Old Testament is the exodus—God's deliverance of his people from political and economic slavery in

Egypt. In the Gospels, Jesus's preferred term of self-identification is "Son of Man"—that is, a "frail, vulnerable human." He is the subject of John's first vision in chapter 1, later reinforced in chapter 14. Readers are to be assured, despite appearances to the contrary, that God rules. Furthermore, God exercises this authority via the very people being squeezed by the powers that be.

This emphasis on "the politics of God" is further developed in the author's vision of the opened heaven in chapter 4, where "throne"—literally, "the seat of power"—is mentioned no less than fifteen times, surely an indication of its importance! Not surprisingly, then, the most common reference to God is to "God the Almighty." Of the ten occurrences of this expression in the New Testament, nine take place in Revelation. It is as if John is saying, "Before I go any further, let me make this point perfectly clear!" Such emphasis is necessary because the earth has become full of counterfeits, frauds, and shams—alternatives that John contrasts in no uncertain terms: an unholy trinity (the devil/dragon, his image, its energizer), animal mascot (beast; chaps. 12–13), urban community (Babylon), and female image for the latter (gaudy prostitute, "loyal" to the highest bidder; chap. 17). In stark opposition stand the Holy Trinity (Father, Son, Spirit), Lamb (chap. 5), new Jerusalem (chaps. 21–22), and bride in white, faithful to her husband (chap. 19). Only with the presentation of such uncompromising choices, free of gray areas, can the deceptive agenda of the devil of "leading astray the entire world" (12:9) be undercut and God's people see things as they really are.

Although God is free to rule directly, without any mediation, the overwhelming divine way of operating according to the Bible has been to entrust day-to-day and age-to-age operations to human agents—especially to the Messiah, the royal and divine Son. However, that mediated rule, that exercise of God's sovereignty, is portrayed by John with mighty but ironic symbols that need to be explained, but in such a way as not to neutralize their raw impact.

The author's effectiveness in illustrating this divine-human strategy can be seen as early as chapter 1. As in all good introductions,

John provides a clue about how to read the following chapters. His first vision (vv. 12–18) is of a glorious figure, whose magnificent and strange features tend to blind most readers to the paradoxes within it. Half of the image resembles a Son of Man: a frail, vulnerable human. He has also experienced the downside of our experience. The other aspect of the picture is of a dazzling supernatural someone—that of God or an angel. God's power is going to be exercised in human weakness.

Other unusual features contribute to the paradox: a two-edged sword is coming out of his mouth—not being held in his hand. While Christian artists through the ages have struggled to keep the scene from looking ridiculous, interpreters have called attention to the profound significance of the weapon's placement: not in the hand. What kind of warfare is going on? What will be the nature of the battles to be fought? Ultimately, the question is one of power, about the nature of God's rule. Can it be that divine power is revealed and exercised by human weakness? Who ever won any conflict by words?

Continuing this theme at 5:1–8, an angel leads John to believe that he is about to see the conquering Lion from the tribe of Judah. Instead, the prophet encounters a Lamb, looking as if its throat had been slit. All that is associated with the power symbolized by the King of beasts, the Lord of the jungle, the Lion King, and King David of the Old Testament is turned upside down and inside out. Conventional views of what it means to be in control are being subverted and redefined. The seven eyes and seven horns are certainly signs of perfect knowing and all strength. However, they are exercised in and through the suffering that sacrifice brings. This victory on earth is celebrated in heaven (vv. 8–14).

Besides creating such symbols, the author adopts, adapts, and arranges images from his Bible, the Christian Old Testament, and from his Eastern Mediterranean environment. Chapter 12 contains clear examples of this "rebirth of images." The ancient political symbol of a dragon is expanded to include a supernatural personage, here named "the devil" and "Satan," and a cosmic scene about war in heaven and a casting down to earth. "That old snake" attempts to devour a magnificent but vulnerable woman in the later stages of labor, who gives birth to a male child. The enemy wants to prevent this Child from "ruling all of the nations" (12:5). An infant in charge of an adult world? How unlikely is that? Were one to pick a single key verse, one could do no better than verse 11: and the brothers and sisters (v. 10) conquered the evil one by the blood of the Lamb and by the word of their own witness, for they loved not their lives—even if it meant death. Once again, lambs don't conquer; dead lambs never win anything.

Finally, there is the Rider on a white horse. Although bearing the title of "King of kings and Lord of lords," he wears a bloody robe: a wounded Warrior who slays the nations by a sword coming from his mouth (19:11–16). Victory is achieved by a war of words, or of "the Word of God" (v. 13)—not by a clash of swords. Apparently, this message was so important (and so difficult to grasp and implement) that John uses the sword image twice: both at the very beginning (chap. 1) and here, near the end. So unconventional are the weapons and methods, so overwhelming are the forces of God and good, that no actual clash of armies is ever described in anything like the detail fantasized by religious novelists, Hollywood screenwriters, or gaming programmers. This is supremely apparent in chapter 16, where the so-called Battle of Armageddon is regularly misnamed. Although occurring at a place called "Armageddon," the text actually refers to the conflict as "battle on the great day of God the Almighty" (v. 14 NRSV). The message seems to be "You can't win, so don't even try." This point is reinforced by the earlier "endings" at 6:12–17; 11:16–20; and 20:1–3. It's also true in the account of the city of Babylon's downfall. Before the Lamb completes Babylon's destruction, she is to be weakened by infighting among her allies—evil feeding on itself (17:15–18). When they are done, that which had seemed so permanent will be proven to be just the opposite—just like every other claim being made: those political and commercial entities that had benefited from this city and empire will lament repeatedly that she was terminated "in one hour" (18:10, 17, 19).

What Do We Learn about Being God's People?

Early in Revelation, John speaks of Jesus having made his followers a "kingdom and priests to God" (1:6; 5:10). This is the political-religious identity and task given first to God's ancient people (Exod. 19:6): to be royal bridge builders, to stand in the gap, to reconcile broken and alienated factions—as a *people collectively* and not only as individuals. Although consisting originally of Israelites, now its membership comprises those from "every tribe, language, people, and nation" (5:9). However, theirs will not be an easy assignment. Followers of the Lamb, last read about in chapters 5 and 12, are more often called "victorious ones" or "conquerors" rather than "believers." Apparently, the latter can be too mental or passive. "Believing" does not convey the cost of being engaged in the struggle against fierce opposition. This defines what it means to be God's child (20:7). The model being held up is none other than Jesus, the reward being to join him on the Father's throne—where he sat down having been an overcomer himself (3:21–22). It is by the witness borne by his followers—even if it means death—and by the Lamb's death that Satan himself *has been*, not will be, defeated (12:11).

That this is no individual experience is signaled early on, the reality being that not every congregation is at the same stage of achievement. Revelation is addressed to the seven churches of Asia, the Roman province in what is now western Turkey—a perfect or complete picture of how the conflict is taking place locally (chaps. 2–3). Only two of them get a clean bill of health: Smyrna (2:8–11) and Philadelphia (3:7–13). Four are both commended and criticized. There is nothing good to say about Laodicea—though the need for and possibility of changing is held out (3:14–22). Although each church is addressed distinctively, at the end of each letter comes the exhortation to everyone, "Hear what the Spirit is

saying to *all* of the churches." Such a range of success and failure
enables Revelation to be read by Christian congregations in analo-
gous circumstances regardless of differences among people, places,
and times. This universality was one of the factors that enabled
Revelation to qualify as a measuring stick—that is, as canonical.

What Do We Learn about God's World?

Because of the pounding that nature takes in Revelation, a reader
could get the impression that God is angry with the way things
have turned out—that creation has become polluted or even that
the world is essentially evil, as some philosophers of the ancient
world used to claim. Some theologians even regard the earth itself
as "fallen." However, a closer reading indicates that one of God's
major strategies is to send a series of shock waves to get the attention of a deceived humanity—the enlisting of God's creation to
cause earth dwellers to "listen up." So the elements of nature are
God's tool, not the target of divine wrath. In fact, the destroyers
of the earth are themselves to be destroyed, according to 11:18!
During the ever-increasing intensity of the seven trumpet blasts and
seven bowl judgments, nature is recruited in the effort to get God's
enemies to repent, to change course—as 9:20–21 and 16:10–11
make abundantly clear. In fact, in the latter passage, the capital
of the evil empire is the bull's-eye. Even its leader is granted the
opportunity to turn toward God. The sentencing phase of God's
judgment is meant to transform rather than to punish—while there
is still time. This is good news indeed. But the heartbreak is that
in neither instance do people repent.

Although nature is good, it had been the stage upon which
evil's influence had been enacted. So the last scene takes place on
a renewed earth, where God wants to be with God's people—a
point made three times (21:1–7), not in a realm beyond the skies.
Just as Babylon was represented as a prostitute decked out in precious stones, so the new Jerusalem, the bride of the Lamb, is by
analogy clothed in streets of gems. This representation of female

urban imagery should neutralize a common expectation of having one's very own mansion on "Gold Boulevard" or "Silver Avenue." With regard to architectural symbolism, there is an unusual aspect to the city's outer perimeter: the presence of both walls and open gates—24/7! At the very least, this means that its citizens are promised both protection and freedom of access.

On the inside, the divine Planner has arranged for the best of two worlds: rural and urban—the finding and renewal of a lost Eden and the establishment of a new Jerusalem, both kinds of human experience being valued. In his commentary on Revelation, Robert W. Wall speaks of the garden as an urban Central Park. The tree of life at the city's downtown, monthly sprouting leaves for the curing of the nations, suggests a progressive, not instantaneous, restoration of nations as well as individuals. The ingrained habits and wounds of millennia need time to be redirected and to heal. Here, then, is a final example of Revelation's transformation of Old Testament images, which locates both Father and Son at the center of a new creation. The grammar of 22:15 suggests that the life God's people enjoy in the new Jerusalem is not limited to some unknown future, even as they pray, "Come, Lord Jesus." Revelation ends with this stunning, hopeful example of the present manifestation of a reality that is yet to appear in its fullness.

$\boxed{11}$

Epilogue

Robert W. Wall

Most of us learn that it's best to read a book from cover to cover, front to back. This is because most plotlines or thesis statements unfold deliberately and logically event by event or proposition by proposition. The design of this book is no different. By following Scripture's final form from cover (Genesis) to cover (Revelation), front (Old Testament) to back (New Testament), we have attempted to introduce readers to a strategy for reading Scripture well. The reason for reading Scripture this way serves mostly theological rather than chronological interests.

Reading Scripture Front to Back

In the first place, Scripture took its final shape one collection at a time, one Testament at a time, to form a single, integral whole. The long history of Scripture's formation indicates that the writings of each collection in each Testament were carefully selected and fitted together at different moments in time, and these different collections were then carefully arranged into a particular sequence in a process that would help secure their ongoing use for holy ends.

By using Scripture's own narrative of God's salvation—its "metanarrative"—to index this book's discussions of each biblical collection, we attempt to guide readers into an unfolding drama in which they themselves are participants. If Scripture is a revelatory text, as we maintain, then this dynamic drama is an indispensable means by which faithful readers learn the truth about God. Biblical stories teach us who God is and the ways God acts in the world.

In fact, the God whom Christians believe is incarnate in Jesus, who is "born to give his disciples second birth," is none other than Israel's God. For this reason, we don't suppose that Scripture's witness to God's self-presentation in the world unfolds in a "progressive" way as though Israel has the first shot at God but doesn't get it quite right or its portrait of God isn't all there. Those who read Scripture in this way tend to marginalize the importance of the Old Testament or even assume that the church has replaced Israel in the economy of God's salvation. Rather, every biblical collection makes its own distinctive contribution to who God is and how God acts, the one complementing the others to form a single, integral word about God.

Pentateuch

Scripture's first few snapshots of God provide cover for every profession Christians make of what is true about God. We meet God actively at work making all things very good and then covenanting with Sarah and Abraham's family to redeem a world that had gone very bad. God is the Creator of all things good but also Savior of all things bad. God is a covenant-making, covenant-keeping God who remembers promises made and keeps them without fail. God is the strangest thing about the Bible precisely because of this: when people fail God, God's mercy remains relentless and on target.

But this doesn't mean God is apathetic when people are faithless. The same God who remembers and rescues Israel from oblivion gets ticked off and needs Moses's convincing to give the next generation of Israelites another chance at succeeding as God's covenant people. God gives Israel a second chance but only after exacting the death sentence on those who disobeyed.

What we find at the beginning of Scripture is the same thing we find at its conclusion: God's final word to creation is a yes, not a no. As creation's sovereign Lord put it to Moses, "This is what 'Lord' means: God is compassionate and merciful, patient and full of great loyalty, faithful to a thousand generations, forgiving every kind of sin and rebellion. But by no means does the Lord clear the guilty: God punishes even the children for their parents' sin to the third and fourth generation" (see Exod. 34:6–7). That's a God who readily forgives but never forgets!

Historical Books

God defines what it means to be God's people on Mount Sinai: God's "most precious possession . . . a kingdom of priests for me and a holy nation" (Exod. 19:5–6 CEB), through whom all the families of earth will be blessed (Gen. 12:3). But there's a catch. In concluding the Pentateuch, Moses prescribes the performance of God's law as the condition and mark of being Israel. God's people have a future only when their covenant-keeping practices witnesses to their partnership with God in saving the world.

The second collection of so-called Historical Books builds upon this foundational witness, repeating the terms of covenant keeping throughout a biblical story that plots Israel's entry into the land as a tribal confederacy and then follows its rise and fall as a misbegotten monarchy. This is a story mostly about God's dealings with a flawed people and failed kingdom whose faithlessness resulted in a divided people and another exile.

Despite the routine failures of Israel's tribal leaders and then its kings to manage the people's covenant with God, King David and, later, the kings Josiah and Hezekiah embody a way forward, a prophetic perspective toward Israel's future. During their rule, God's Torah is elevated not only to guide a people's conduct but also to form their collective understanding of God and themselves as a "holy nation" through whom the families of earth will be blessed. Before his spiritual failure, Solomon also secured the importance of wisdom as a complement to the Torah, while the Chronicler's David (along with Josiah) added the importance of a community's worship of God to its religious curriculum. A nation cannot become holy without it also becoming a "kingdom of priests."

This is the organizing vision for a postexilic Israel under the leadership of Ezra and Nehemiah. Even though at the bidding of a pagan monarch (Cyrus), they instituted a limited but pivotal role for this renewed Israel as caretaker for the coming of creation's messianic Lord, Jesus. It is he who will lead God's people into the future God has ordained; he will exercise his rule by the light of the Torah, complemented by biblical wisdom and worship, all of which is interpreted and incarnated by the risen One.

Wisdom/Poetry Books

Before he is corrupted by political ambition, the young Solomon understands well the importance of wisdom and worship for directing an obedience of God's Torah that forges a faithful partnership with God. At the center of biblical wisdom and the community's book of worship (the Psalter) is a robust vision of God's providential care of creation. It is this theological vision that animates Israel's forward movement into God's future.

This is precisely the question posed of God by Job in response to his suffering, which is a mystery to Job and his friends. God's self-presentation in the whirlwind is as much a reminder as a revelation: the Creator's nature lesson makes sense of a world that is ordered by God, grants freedom, and allows mystery while also receiving God's care, which is anything but random or arbitrary. Things do go wrong; bad things can happen to good people. But

Job reminds us that a holy negotiation of life's hardships and heartbreaks requires a careful look into the real world God has made good.

Ecclesiastes makes a similar point in the face of a similar skepticism but drills down on what can be learned by more critical observations of a life well lived. The pairing of Job and Ecclesiastes, which engenders confidence in God's eternal order, is placed alongside of proverbial wisdom whose humanistic orientation underscores the confidence the Creator vests in people just like Job and Qoheleth—in other words, wise people whose fidelity to God enables them to discern straight paths from crooked in the way forward.

The Psalms shift the reader's focus from Job's hard questions and the Creator's equally demanding response—which concern human experience of the natural order—to the spiritual order forged by worshiping God in every circumstance. This collection teaches the reader that a fully formed life requires attention to both witnesses. And both witnesses are necessary in confirming that God's instruction is tried and true (Prov. 30:4).

Prophetic Books

The collection of prophetic books comes last in the Old Testament and for good reason: prophets are the carriers of God's Word who look back on a history of Israel's failure to keep its covenant with God, which occasions a justifiable punishment (e.g., exile). But prophets also carry a word of hope about Israel's future restoration and a new exodus to a new Jerusalem at the center of a new creation. Ezekiel speaks of a new temple, while Jeremiah speaks of a new covenant when worship and obedience are gladly given God.

The Book of the Twelve calls salvation's endgame "the day of the Lord," when Sinai's promise of a holy nation and kingdom of priests is realized. Then Israel will truly be Israel, a beacon of light to all nations. In that moment at the end of salvation's history, God's holiness, which demands a particular people's faithfulness, and God's grace, which extends to the repair of all nations and nature—the central dialectic of the prophetic word—come together to form an everlasting synthesis.

But from the prophets' vantage point, this grand moment still lies in the future. Their word provides the inertia for Israel's forward movement—but it is still forward and not final. What comes next in the Bible's story tells of Israel's destiny when the goal of its history is identified as the Son of God, Messiah, Jesus, in whom the multilayered newness promised by the prophets is realized (cf. Rom. 10:4).

The Four Gospels

The fourfold Gospel tells the authorized biography of Jesus; his life is Scripture's climax because through his life the truth about God is witnessed in a person. The Gospel is the reader's plumb line; keep its plotline and its characterization of the risen (i.e., living) Jesus ever before you! After all, he is the bread of life, the light of the world. What comes before the Gospel in the Old Testament and after it in the New Testament is interpreted by and in turn interprets all the rest. The church's ancient practice of using a lectionary of readings to guide a congregation's hearing of the Bible in worship gets this right (see below). The traditional offices occupied by the risen Christ—prophet, priest, king, and sage—are yet another way of imagining this same point: the various Old Testament collections, and the variety of witnesses each includes, aim readers ahead to the Gospel story of Jesus.

Even though the relationship between Jesus and his Father is the Gospel's pivot point, the Lord's relationship with his disciples is also crucial for the reader to follow. Even though the biblical story of Israel in many ways resonates with Jesus, so too does the story of his disciples. In various ways, the disciples, like Israel, embody the promise (e.g., capacity to love enemies) and all the problems (e.g., faithlessness, hypocrisy) of their holy calling to live in a manner worthy of citizenship in God's kingdom.

Acts and the Letters

Some skeptics still wonder whether Jesus was a "one-off"—a charismatic flash in the pan who is done and gone. Perhaps a response to this skepticism is latent in the Gospel's concluding "great commission": those who witness the risen Jesus and who, with Thomas, confess him as Lord and God are ordered to continue to do and say what Jesus began. But nothing is said about whether the Lord's command to continue is obeyed. Acts responds that the promised Spirit ascends and fills up his followers to enable them to obey the risen Jesus. Even though he is the risen Lord, he is no one-off; his mission continues in his absence under the power of God's Spirit. The promises God makes to Israel according to Scripture continue to be realized mission by mission to the end of the earth.

The two collections of apostolic letters, Pauline and Catholic, operationalize in concrete terms—through their instruction, exhortation, and theological explanation—what is introduced in Acts. The narrative world of Acts arranges the missions and their respective apostolic leaders in ways that are suggestive of the working relationship between the two collections of letters. At the same time, the reader of Acts is well prepared for the crises that typically occasion a reading of the letters: theological error, intramural conflicts, instructions that guide the worship and missionary practices of the congregation, and so on. Acts also cues Old Testament texts by citation and allusion that expand the reader's preparation for reading the letters (Acts 2:17–21; 15:16–17; 28:26–27).

Hardly another theme is more important in the letters than apostolic leadership. Most Pauline letters are generally concerned to defend Paul's apostolicity and his personal importance for the church's future; however, his so-called Pastoral Letters (1–2 Timothy, Titus) are more concerned with the transmission of Paul's settled apostolic legacy to the next generation. This also seems to be the case with the Catholic Epistles, whose implied authors are eyewitnesses of the incarnate Word (see 1 John 1:1–4). This concern for an apostolic succession that moves the testimony of truth and love from one generation to the next clears away the brush for the church's forward movement toward the salvation now realized in heaven but not yet on earth.

The Revelation to Saint John

The final placement of Revelation at Scripture's end provides an apt visual aid of the role it performs as Scripture's concluding chapter. Revelation is read last not only to give the reader heaven's perspective on all that has happened during the course of salvation's history; it is read last to assure the reader of God's final victory over all those deadly forces that oppose God's eternal reign as Creator who created all things according to God's will (cf. Rev. 4:11).

At the center of Revelation's vision of the last days is the same one whose gospel stands at the center of Scripture: the exalted Jesus. He is called many things in this book: "faithful witness," "alpha and omega," "Lamb," "Lion," "King of kings, Lord of lords," and still other metaphors that set out the scope and result of his messianic mission. We are reminded that it is by God's partnership with a wounded warrior (whose sword comes from his mouth) that the world now ruled by an unholy trinity will be replaced by a new world populated by a global community of Lamb followers who encircle the Holy Trinity in worship and praise going forward into eternity. So Scripture concludes not with a whimper but with an awe-inspiring apocalypse of God's salvation.

Reading Scripture Back to Front

As important as it is to learn to read Scripture as an unfolding story from front (Pentateuch) to back (Revelation), it is also important to learn to read Scripture from back to front! Throughout this book mention is made of how biblical texts recall other biblical texts, whether by citation or allusion, to amplify or clarify the meaning of one text by an appeal to another.

This literary phenomenon, which even the first interpreters of Scripture employed, is more recently called **intertextuality**. A study of Scripture's intertextuality typically concentrates on the working relationship between different biblical texts, and even between biblical and related nonbiblical texts. Biblical texts should never be read in isolation from other biblical texts; the interdependency of the diverse parts of Scripture is characteristic of its overall unity. Careful readers note the "canon consciousness" of different writers who routinely quote specific verses from their Bibles (sometimes in revised form) to tell their stories or score their points. Close analysis of these "intertexts" that link together earlier texts from the writer's Scriptures with those they have written is one way of reading Scripture from back to front.

While biblical writers often have earlier biblical texts in mind when composing their stories or letters, Scripture's intertextuality is also a property of its canonization. We might allow that the Holy Spirit, who guided the church's formation of Scripture, had certain inspired intertexts in mind that are embedded in Scripture's final form and are now recognized by careful readers. Scripture's robust intertextuality, which extends to collections as well as particular pairs of texts, is a property of a single biblical canon, the production of "one body and one Spirit" (Eph. 4:4), and not of the authors/editors of those texts and collections. For this reason, our study of these various relationships, especially between canonical collections, follows the *church's* intention for its Scripture, which is to use it for forming the saving wisdom of God's people and equipping the church for the good life of serving God (cf. 2 Tim. 3:15–17).

Every chapter of this book mentions a variety of connections between canonical collections, and sometimes between different books within each collection. Every chapter asks readers to practice making these connections in profitable ways. For example, the close relationship within the Pentateuch between Genesis and Exodus establishes the connection between creation's beginning and the beginning of Israel as the covenant community promised to Abraham (see Gen. 12:1–3) and made good on Mount Sinai (see Exod. 19). And what about the order of Old Testament Wisdom books, which proceeds from Job's story that puzzles over why bad things sometimes happen to good people before raising a series of responses to this hard question that are found in the Psalms and Proverbs? The chapter on Acts and the letters makes clear the working relationship between these biblical books.

The most important relationship created by the formation of the church's Scripture, of course, is between the Old and New Testaments. Much is made about the nature of their relationship as different witnesses to the one and only God. Different chapters have hinted at ways of defining this pivotal dialogue. Most common is to think of the Old Testament—which concludes with the collection of prophetic books that promises a restored Israel, a renewed covenant, and a new creation—as continuing into the New, which appropriately begins with a fourfold Gospel that plots the story of the resurrected Messiah through whom God fulfills the promises made to Israel according to Scripture.

Readers may also recognize that the addition of a second Testament to the first creates a chiasm that pairs the Bible's beginning (creation) with its conclusion (new creation) and the historical books that tell of Israel's beginning, complemented by the poets, sages, and prophets, with the historical book that tells of the church's beginning (Acts), complemented by apostolic letters. Both these pairs encircle what stands at Scripture's epicenter, the story's climax and center of reference: the incarnation of God's Son, Jesus, whose life is lived as a ransom for many. Some church traditions help us visualize this theologic by the lectionary, which combines Old Testament and New Testament readings, often with a psalm sung or read responsively, before hearing the Gospel lesson read as the reference point for all Scripture.

This textbook has followed a "metanarrative"—a sweeping cover story that loops the diverse parts as indispensable elements of the biblical whole. The danger of this way of putting things together is that the inertia is always forward from beginning to conclusion. Inevitably this way of reading privileges the New over the Old. "Old" becomes a metaphor for things already read, already completed with value only as a memory of a strange past, Israel's past. But, as William Faulkner put it so well, "the past is never dead. It's not even past."

Although readers should keep the Gospel's narrative of Jesus's life, death, and resurrection always in mind when studying Scripture, since the incarnation is Scripture's constant reference point; it also is true that readers should keep the Old Testament narrative of Israel always in mind when studying the Gospel's narrative of Jesus! Jesus demonstrates that Israel's "past is never dead. It's not even past."

Learning to Read Scripture Well: Next Steps

Cultivating the practices that enable one to read Scripture well, whether from front to back or back to front, requires both work and worship. The intellectual work involved targets knowing what Scripture says. Wrapping the biblical text in its various contexts for sound interpretation involves knowing something about the circumstances of its composition and canonization. The careful reader should also extend this context to engage the long history of its interpretation by God's people and within culture.

This textbook just sets the table for a feast of many courses. We haven't been very interested in the historian's work, which seeks to reconstruct the ancient (and strange!) world that comes with the Bible. Other textbooks will need to do this heavy lifting. Frankly, we believe the hard work of historians, while important, often creates a distance between Scripture and its current readers and setting. This is a *canonical* book that purposes to address all God's people where they live with a word from God that's on target. The aim of biblical interpretation is to hear that word.

Only rarely have we treated specific biblical texts in detail. Any careful reader will need to practice the tools of the trade on biblical texts; it's our desire that this textbook be used to complement such a study. Simply put, the immediate aim of good interpretation is to know what a biblical text plainly says. Beyond the theological introduction to canonical collections provided by this book, an introductory course in Scripture should have as its primary outcome making students alert to the importance of words and their grammatical relationship with other words set within a composition that tells a story, sings a lyric, makes an argument, or envisions a future with God. The Bible is a sacred text, inspired by God's Spirit for Christian formation. This belief alone should motivate the most careful study of the biblical text. The faithful reader should never tire of gathering more information that will help her or him know the text inside and out.

The reader's intellectual formation is only one element of what is needed. Because the primary purpose of Bible study is to know God, one's spiritual preparation is also crucial in meeting this goal. The reader should know the text well; but she or he should also know God well. This is why the hard work of our intellectual formation should be accompanied by worship and prayer.

Our hope is that this textbook has enriched your study of Scripture. We hope that your study doesn't stop here, but that it has only increased your desire to know God better. The persistent practice of reading and rereading Scripture—all of it, forward and backward, hunting down solid answers to hard questions asked of it, investigating and using what you find there in the struggles of daily life—will continue to form in faithful readers a Spirit-fed wisdom and moral maturity that enables their full participation with God in the renewal of all things for Christ's sake.

Glossary

Alexander the Great (356–323 BCE): The Greek conqueror who, in just over a decade, amassed an enormous empire that included the land formerly belonging to Israel. *See also* **Hellenism, Hellenization.**

allegory: A form of reading that understands features of texts to symbolize spiritual realities, under the assumption that God seeks to reveal deeper things to the reader that are not obviously present in the "literal sense" of the text.

Antiochus IV (215–164 BCE): Seleucid king whose oppression against Jews (including the desecration of the temple and the outlawing of Judaism) helped bring about the **Maccabean Revolt.**

apocalypse: From the Greek *apocalypsis*, literally meaning "unveiling," but understood to mean "revelation." *See also* **revelation.**

Apocrypha, apocryphal: From a Greek word meaning "hidden"; refers to ancient literature not accepted as fully canonical in the collection of Jewish or Christian Scriptures. Among these texts are those designated "deuterocanonical" in the Roman Catholic tradition. *See also* **Deuterocanon, deuterocanonical.**

apostle: From the Greek meaning "one sent" as an emissary or ambassador. Early Christians reserved the term for those who had received a commission to ministry from the risen Christ. *See also* **disciple, discipleship.**

ark of the covenant: A religious object that evokes the presence and power of God. Sometimes sacred objects are placed in it (e.g., the tablets of the covenant). The ark is typically mobile.

Assyria: An ancient Mesopotamian empire existing from ca. 2500 to 605 BCE. Assyria was responsible for conquering the northern kingdom of Israel in 722 BCE and dispersing its inhabitants throughout the Assyrian Empire (1 Kings 17). *See also* **Diaspora, dispersion.**

Babylon: An ancient Mesopotamian city-state that achieved empire status at first in the second millennium BCE, and again later as the "Neo-Babylonian Empire" from 608 to 539 BCE. Babylon was responsible for the conquering of the southern kingdom of Judah in 587 BCE, the destruction of Solomon's temple in Jerusalem, and the deportation of the majority of its people back to the city of Babylon. *See also* **exile.**

baptism: The Christian ritual of initiation, practiced according to Jesus's command (Matt. 28:18–20), whereby individuals are plunged in water to signify either repentance (in the case of John the Baptist) or participation in the death and resurrection of Jesus. *See also* **sacrament, sacramental.**

BCE, CE: "Before the Common Era" and "Common Era" are frequent replacements for "BC" ("Before Christ") and "AD" (*anno domini,* "in the year of our Lord"), which indicate dates prior to and after the birth of Jesus.

benediction: A blessing in the form of an invocation of God's help and guidance, typically coming at the end of a religious act, whether a worship service or a Christian letter.

Book of the Twelve: The last book of the **canonical prophets,** so called because the twelve short writings (Hosea–Malachi) would fit on a single scroll. They are often designated the Minor Prophets to distinguish them from the much longer "major" prophetic books of Isaiah, Jeremiah, Ezekiel, and Daniel.

Canaanites: A term that sometimes refers to a particular group and sometimes to the collective inhabitants of the land that Israel was to occupy. When the term refers to the latter, the so-called Seven Nations are often specified (Hittites, Girgashites, Amorites, Canaanites, Perizzites, Hivites, and Jebusites).

canon, canonical, canonization: From a Greek word meaning "measure," "canon" referred initially to a "rule" (as in a ruler with which one measures) but came to also refer to an official, approved list. Authorized persons, doctrines, and books can be designated "canonical." Typically "canon" and "canonical" refer to the collection of Christian

Scriptures, and "canonization" refers to the process by which those books were collected into an authoritative whole.

canonical prophets: Prophets of Israel who have books named after them in the Bible. The Prophets make up the fourth canonical collection of the Christian Old Testament and the second of three canonical units of the Jewish Bible. *See also* **prophet.**

catholic: From a Greek word meaning "whole" or "universal." When capitalized, it typically refers to the Roman Catholic Church. When not capitalized, it refers to the ancient tradition of Christianity characterized by a devotion to unity, an embrace of limited but real diversity, and an aversion to division. "Catholicity" is recognized as one of the four classic marks of the Christian church according to the Nicene Creed: "We believe in one holy *catholic* and apostolic church." *See also* **Catholic Epistles.**

Catholic Epistles: The New Testament letter collection including one letter from Jesus's brother James, two from the apostle Peter, three from the apostle John, and one from Jesus's brother Jude—figures associated with the mission to Jews in Jerusalem and designated "pillars" of that church by Paul (Gal. 2:9). The ancient church called these letters "catholic" in part because most of them bear a "universal" address. Evidence also exists that the letters were included to ensure the "catholicity" of the apostolic message—that is, to balance out the immense impact of Paul's witness in order to ensure the New Testament included a "whole" communication from all of the apostles and not just Paul alone.

church fathers: Leaders of the ancient Christian church who lived after the time of the apostles and were recognized as great teachers or influential bishops.

circumcision: The sign of the covenant with God for Jewish males, performed on the eighth day of life, wherein the foreskin of the penis is removed.

consummation: The point at which something is considered complete or finalized. In the biblical metanarrative, the "consummation" refers to the completion of God's redemptive work at the end of time.

covenant: A relational promise or treaty between two parties. In the Bible, covenants are established between God and God's people that set out the terms of their relationship.

Cyrus of Persia (600 or 576 to 530 BCE): King of the Persian Empire who conquered Babylon in 538 BCE and allowed the Jews in exile there to return to their homeland.

Dead Sea Scrolls: Ancient manuscripts discovered in the mid-twentieth century in caves near the Dead Sea. The texts found there were once in the library of the Qumran community, which dwelled nearby from the second century BCE until the Roman conquest during the First Jewish War (66–74 CE). The discovery was a major find insofar as the library included manuscripts of the Old Testament as well as the writings of a Jewish messianic sect roughly contemporaneous with earliest Christianity. *See also* **Essenes.**

Deuterocanon, deuterocanonical: The Roman Catholic title for biblical books frequently called "Apocrypha" by Protestants. As the name makes plain, deuterocanonical texts hold a "secondary" level of canonical authority. *See also* **Apocrypha, apocryphal.**

Diaspora, dispersion: From a Greek word meaning "scatter," "diaspora" bears both geographical and theological meanings in the Bible. Geographically, the Diaspora referred to the places outside the land of Palestine to which Jews had been "scattered," but it also functioned theologically in reference to believers scattered away from their true spiritual home (be that Jerusalem or the kingdom of God) and living as aliens and exiles in a foreign land as a result. *See also* **exile.**

disciple, discipleship: From a Greek word meaning "learner" or "apprentice," "disciple" is used to designate a follower of Jesus.

eschatology, eschatological: The theology of last or final things that describes God's goal for creation.

Essenes: A sectarian group in first-century Judaism dedicated to spiritual purity and strict conformity to the Jewish law. The Essenes believed the temple in Jerusalem had been corrupted by Hellenistic influences and thus withdrew from it. Many scholars today associate the Essenes with the Qumran community. *See also* **Dead Sea Scrolls.**

exile: A stock term usually referring to the Babylonian destruction of Judah in 587 BCE. However, the northern kingdom of Israel also suffered an exile previously in 722 BCE at the hand of the Assyrians. *See also* **Diaspora, dispersion.**

gentile(s): A term referring to the nations other than Israel or persons who are not ethnically Jewish.

gospel: From the Greek term *euangelion*, meaning "good news," "gospel" referred initially to preaching the life, death, and resurrection of Jesus. Later it came to function also as a genre of literature focused on the person and teaching of Jesus. The four Gospels make up the first canonical unit of the New Testament.

Hebrew poetry: Known primarily by its parallel members, in which thoughts more than sounds rhyme. All of the Psalter, most of the prophets, and a few other large books (e.g., Job, Proverbs) are written in poetic form.

Hellenism, Hellenization: A term referring to the larger Greek culture that dominated the Mediterranean and eastward world after the conquest of Alexander the Great (356–323 BCE). Hellenization made Greek the common tongue of the day and introduced aspects of Greek culture to the peoples and religions affected.

Herod the Great, Herodians: Herod the Great (ca. 74–4 BCE) was the Roman client king of Judea referred to in Gospel accounts of Jesus's birth (e.g., Matt. 2). By Jesus's adult years Judea was divided among his sons (Luke 3:1). The Herodians referred to in the Gospels could have been courtiers or soldiers of Herod but were probably a political party of sorts distinguishable from the two major parties of the day, the Pharisees and the Sadducees. *See also* **Pharisees**; **Sadducees**.

historical: Describing intellectual inquiry into the cause and effects of human action in space and time. While human history may be conceived as the sum total of human experience, that is ultimately a history that only God knows. What human beings regard as historical is limited to human action and reaction as discernible from documentation and made public and subject to review, criticism, and improvement.

hyperbole: The rhetorical use of exaggeration as a figure of speech designed to make a powerful impression, but not to be taken literally. Jesus is speaking hyperbolically, for instance, when he insists that his followers must "hate" their family members if they want to be his followers (e.g., Luke 14:26).

intertestamental period: The period in Israel's history from the time of the second temple's construction in the sixth century BCE to its destruction in 70 CE.

intertextuality: Refers to expanding the meaning of a text by relating it to other biblical (and sometimes nonbiblical) texts that use similar words and ideas.

judges: Leaders called by God to deliver Israel from oppression, even though the oppression came about by Israel's sin. Israel's judges are major characters in the Old Testament books leading up to the rise of the monarchy (i.e., Joshua–1 Samuel).

kingdom of God: The place, or situation, where God's rule is acknowledged and God's will is accomplished.

Lord's Supper: A ritual practiced by Christians, by Jesus's command (e.g., Matt. 26:26–29; 1 Cor. 11:23–26), to memorialize Christ's death, celebrate Christian fellowship, and anticipate the great feast that will take place at Christ's return. *See also* **sacrament, sacramental**.

Maccabean Revolt (167–160 BCE): A rebellion against the Jews' Seleucid overlords that resulted in a brief independence for the Jewish people. So named after Mattathias the Hasmonean's eldest son, Judas Maccabeus (i.e., Judas "the Hammer"), who led the revolution following his father's death. Under Judas's leadership, the Jewish rebels eventually recaptured parts of Jerusalem (164 BCE), rededicating the temple to God and restoring the Jewish practices Antiochus had banned. The Jewish community still celebrates this improbable victory at the Festival of Lights, called "Hanukkah."

messiah: The term means "anointed," typically with (olive) oil. This sacred act indicates divine selection for a certain task, such as prophet or king. The Greek term is *Christ*.

metanarrative: A grand, overarching story that takes a group of smaller, different stories and provides a framework for understanding how they all fit together.

Moabite: Generally, the term refers to a particular population and nation-state that abutted Israel. More important, the term is derisive in that the story telling of the origins of the Moabites (and Ammonites) is a sordid account of incest (Gen. 19:30–38). This is what makes the story of Ruth the Moabite so radical.

parable: A story, saying, or riddle that compares something—often from nature—with the kingdom of God, in order to illustrate what the kingdom is about or to point to who God is. As such, Jesus's parables typically challenge standard worldviews and shock with the radical logic of God's ways.

Passover: The annual Jewish commemoration of their deliverance by God from slavery in Egypt (see Exod. 12).

Pentateuch: The first "five books" of the Old Testament, called the "Torah" in Judaism and the Hebrew Scriptures (Josh. 1:7–8). The Pentateuch is the first canonical unit of the Old Testament, containing both narrative and legal texts. *See also* **Torah.**

Pentecost: A Jewish agricultural festival known in the Old Testament as the "Feast of Weeks" or "Feast of the Harvest," one of three major festivals of the Jewish year (see, e.g., Exod. 23:14–17). In the New Testament book of Acts, the outpouring of the Holy Spirit on believers took place during the celebration of this festival in Jerusalem (Acts 2).

Pharisees: A first-century movement of laymen (nonpriests) who were focused on preserving the purity of Jewish religious practice against the defilements of Greek and Roman culture. Made up of teachers and experts in the law (rabbis and scribes), this is the group most closely associated with Jesus and therefore comprises his primary antagonists in the Gospel narratives.

prescript: The opening section of a Greco-Roman letter that identifies the author and sender and concludes with a greeting.

priest: A human who mediates between God and humanity, especially in the offering of sacrifices. In ancient Israel such persons led Israel in its worship of God and served as advisors and leaders.

proem: A part of the opening section of a Greco-Roman letter coming after the prescript, typically including expressions of joy, thanksgiving, and prayers for the recipient. The proem was included to ensure a warm reception of the letter's content and often hints at the main themes of the letter body.

promised land: Refers to Canaan, the land specifically promised to the ancestors of Israel as related in Genesis 12–50.

prophet: A specialized spokesperson for God. In the Old Testament, various prophets appear in Joshua, Judges, Samuel, Kings, and Chronicles. The title is not sufficient, however, since these stories also include the presence of false prophets. Persons designated as prophets also appear in the New Testament (e.g., Matt. 11:9; Luke 2:36; Acts 15:32) and, as in the Old Testament, there are false prophets among them (e.g., Matt. 7:15; Acts 13:6; 1 John 4:1). *See also* **canonical prophets.**

Psalms: Songs and liturgies that are a central part of the prayer and worship of Jews and Christians. The Old Testament book of Psalms is a five-part collection including psalms of thanksgiving, praise, lament, and confession.

reconciliation: The restoration of right relations. Often synonymous with "atonement," an Old English word referring to the *at-one-ment* created when a broken relationship is restored.

redeem, redemption: Literally to gain or regain possession of something by offering a payment. Biblically the word is used most frequently in relation to God's deliverance of Israel from slavery in Egypt and the deliverance of all humanity from the effects of human sin through Jesus's work of reconciliation.

revelation: The act of revealing something. In the Bible, "revelation" may refer to God's self-revealing in the act of creation, in God's relationship with the people of Israel, and, principally, in the work of Jesus Christ. The final book of the Bible, called the "Revelation to John" or the "Apocalypse of John," contains a vision of God's **consummation** received by a disciple named John while in exile on the island of Patmos.

righteous: A term referring to the high moral character of the person who lives in right relationship with God.

sacrament, sacramental: Traditionally defined as an outward and visible sign of an inward and spiritual grace. In a sacrament, God takes ordinary, mundane things (like water, bread, and wine) and accomplishes extraordinary things through them. The two "dominical" sacraments (so named because they were commanded by the Lord) are baptism and the Lord's Supper. *See also* **baptism; Lord's Supper.**

Sadducees: One of the dominant sects of first-century Judaism, made up of the priestly class and those particularly associated with the temple in Jerusalem. In contrast to the Pharisees, the Sadducees recognized only the Torah as authoritative Scripture.

Samaria: An ancient city and mountain in northern Palestine that served as the capital of the northern kingdom of Israel. In Jesus's day it was the place of devotion for the Samaritans. *See also* **Samaritans.**

Samaritans: Inhabitants of the ancient northern kingdom of Israel who in Jesus's day were rivals of Jews associated with the Jerusalem temple. Pious Jews considered them to be religiously impure and thus had no dealings with them.

Sanhedrin: An aristocratic council presided over by the Jewish high priest to which Rome entrusted some aspects of local government.

scribes: A writer and copier of manuscripts. In the Gospels, the scribes are associated with the Pharisees and may be thought of as lawyers or experts in the law.

Septuagint: The Greek translation of the Jewish Scriptures produced as a product of Hellenization in the third and fourth centuries BCE. The name derives from a tradition of the "seventy" scribes who performed the work. This Greek version of the Hebrew texts functioned as the authoritative Scriptures for earliest Christians and continues as the basis for biblical texts of Christian groups associated with Eastern Orthodoxy.

synagogue: From a Greek word meaning "gather together" or "assembly," the synagogue developed in the postexilic period as a place where Jews living away from Jerusalem might gather together for prayers and the reading of Scripture.

Torah: The Hebrew name (Josh. 1:7–8) for the first five books of the Old Testament. Meaning "instruction" in Hebrew, the word is also sometimes used to designate the whole instruction of God derived from the Scriptures. The Torah includes both narratives and the law of Moses.

transhistorical: Refers to human actions in space and time in which God is also involved. This is the main category for biblical material since the main actor in the Bible is God. Divine action cannot be ascertained by the normal rules of historical research.

Vulgate: The Latin translation of the Bible produced by Jerome and his school at the end of the fourth century CE. The Vulgate served as the authoritative version of the Bible for the Western church and continues to serve as the basis for versions of the Bible considered authoritative for Roman Catholics.

wisdom: A way of life dependent on observing how the world in all its dimensions (e.g., political, social, religious, familial, economic) works and then acting appropriately. Wisdom that comes from God combines this feature with the necessity of obeying God as well. There is a downside to wisdom when it is used for self-aggrandizement.

Wisdom literature: A term referring to Old Testament books of wisdom, principally Job, Proverbs, and Ecclesiastes, along with the Wisdom of Solomon and Sirach in the **Deuterocanon.**

Writings: The third canonical unit of both the Jewish Bible and the Christian Old Testament. In Jewish Bibles it is the final collection and contains many more books than the Christian Old Testament, which includes only books of wisdom and poetry—Job, Psalms, Proverbs, Ecclesiastes, and Song of Songs.

Yahweh: The personal name of the Creator God of Israel as revealed to Moses (Exod. 3:14; 6:2–3). This crucially important name for God occurs around sixty-eight hundred times in the Old Testament and was considered so sacred that ancient scribes replaced it with *Adonai*, rendered "Lord" in English translations. The name itself appears to be a derivative of the Hebrew "to be" verb, so it is typically taken to mean something like "I am."

Zealots: A sect of first-century Judaism that strove for military victory over Rome and the reestablishment of the Jewish nation.

List of Contributors

Daniel Castelo (PhD, Duke University) is associate professor of theology at Seattle Pacific University. He is the author of *The Apathetic God* and other books.

Laura C. S. Holmes (PhD, Princeton Theological Seminary) is assistant professor of New Testament at Seattle Pacific University. She is the author of *The Theological Role of Paradox in the Gospel of Mark*.

Sara Koenig (PhD, Princeton Theological Seminary) is associate professor of biblical studies at Seattle Pacific University. She is the author of *Isn't This Bathsheba? A Study in Characterization*.

Eugene E. Lemcio (PhD, Cambridge University) is professor emeritus of New Testament at Seattle Pacific University. He is the author of *Navigating Revelation: Charts for the Voyage* and other books.

Bo Lim (PhD, Trinity Evangelical Divinity School) is associate professor of Old Testament at Seattle Pacific University. He is the author of *The "Way of the Lord" in the Book of Isaiah*.

Chad Marshall (PhD, Princeton Theological Seminary) is instructor of Christian Scripture at Seattle Pacific University.

David R. Nienhuis (PhD, University of Aberdeen) is associate professor of New Testament Studies at Seattle Pacific University. He is the author of *Not by Paul Alone: The Formation of the Catholic Epistle Collection and the Christian Canon.*

Frank Anthony Spina (PhD, University of Michigan) is professor of Old Testament at Seattle Pacific University. He is the author of *The Faith of the Outsider: Exclusion and Inclusion in the Biblical Story.*

Robert W. Wall (ThD, Dallas Theological Seminary) is Paul T. Walls Professor of Scripture and Wesleyan Studies at Seattle Pacific University. He is the author of numerous books and commentaries on the New Testament, including, with David Nienhuis, *Reading the Epistles of James, Peter, John, and Jude as Scripture: The Shaping and Shape of a Canonical Collection.*

Index